KU-106-061

Facts about

FINLAND

17th revised edition

Kustannusosakeyhtiö Otava
Otava Publishing Company Ltd.
Helsinki 1981

Edited by Jyrki Leskinen

Photographs: Mauri Korhonen, Lehtikuva Oy, Aulis Nyqvist,
Otava Publishing Company Ltd, Ritva Räty, Esa Santakari,
Erkki Talvila

ISBN 951-1-06638-2

Kustannusosakeyhtiö Otavan painolaitokset
Keuruu 1981
Printed in Finland

CONTENTS

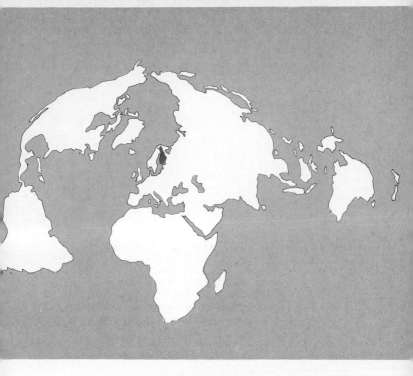

THE LAND AND THE PEOPLE

Finland (Suomi) is, after Iceland, the most northerly
country in the world. About one third of its total length
lies north of the Arctic Circle.

Geographic position: between lats. 59° 30' 10" and 70°
05' 30" N and longs. 19° 07' 03" and 31° 35' 20" E. Total
area: 337,032 sq. km.

Maximum length: 1,160 km, maximum width 540 km.
Coast line: 1,100 km.

Frontier: with Sweden 586 km, with Norway 716 km,
with the USSR 1,269 km; total 2,571 km.

Population: 4,788,000. Density of population: 15.6 per
sq. km.

Topography

The soil is mainly moraine deposits left by ice age
glaciers. It is usually so thin that the topography follows

the contours of the archaean bedrock. Most of the country is low, rising gradually in the SSW−NNE direction up to the fell districts of Lapland. But it is not flat lowland type. It is heavily broken up with rocky outcrops, ridges, valleys and hollows which usually contain lakes.

Seas and Inland Waters

Finland is bounded by the Gulf of Bothnia and the Gulf of Finland. There are about 30,000 islands off the Finnish coast, mainly in the south and south-west. The 60,000 lakes comprise 9 % of the total area. In the great lake districts of the interior water covers 20−50 % of the surface.

Climate

Owing to the Gulf Stream and general air currents, average temperatures in Finland are considerably higher at all seasons than in other countries at the same latitude. Finland is in the snow and forest zone, characterized by warm summers and cold winters. South Finland has 19 hours of daylight at Midsummer. In North Finland, which starts just below the Arctic Circle, there is perpetual daylight for 73 days at the 70th parallel in summer and 51 days of unending night around Christmas.

Summer, with a mean temperature of 50 °C (10 °F) lasts for 110−122 days in the south and 50−85 days in the north. The country is snow-covered for about 5 months of the year in the south and up to 7 months in Lapland.

Temperatures: July (mean): 55−63 °F (13−17 °C) (maximum): 86 °F (30 °C). February (mean): +26 °F to −7 °F (−3 °C to −14 °C) (minimum): below −22 °F (−30 °C).

Annual precipitation (rain and snow): SW Finland: 27″ (700 mm), NW Finland (Lapland): 16″ (400 mm).

Flora and Fauna

Finland is situated almost entirely in the northern zone of coniferous forests. The oak zone in the south-west and along the south coast, however, is almost Central European in type. In Lapland, proceeding north, spruce is the first tree species to disappear, followed by pine; the timber line is generally formed by dwarf birch. The flora is richest in South Finland, particularly in the Åland Islands.

There are 67 species of mammal native to Finland. Nowadays bears and wolves are found only in the eastern frontier districts and the wilds of Lapland, where there are also great herds of reindeer. There are over 100,000 elk. The commonest furbearing animals are the red squirrel, musk-rat, pinemarten and fox. Game birds — grouse, wild duck, capercaillie, blackcock and ptarmigan — are plentiful. The rivers and lakes are full of fish; the rivers of Lapland are famed for their salmon.

Nature Conservation and Environmental Protection

The environmental problem caused by forestry and the use of forests is reflected at many levels in Finnish society. Forests are the main recreational sites, the most important scenic factor, the source of many by-products such as berries, mushrooms, lichen, game and reindeer meat, and above all they are the living environment of various animal and plant species. Multiple use of the forests is safeguarded by the most versatile possible protection, care and use of not only the growing stock but of the biocoenosis.

Finland has 20 national parks and 20 nature parks totalling about 5,475 sq.km. The picture is from Lammi, the primeval forest area of Evo.

85—90 % of the waterways are still unpolluted but approximately half of the population lives on unclean water systems. The share of the forest industry in direct biological oxygen consumption is 85 %, that of settlement only 9 %. Municipal wastes load the water systems, causing eutrophication and so-called secondary oxygen consumption. Water systems are protected by developing industrial converting processes that consume as little water as possible, and waste waters are purified as effectively as possible. The purification of municipal effluent is also being improved steadily. The character

of the waterways has also been altered by harnessing them for the production of hydroelectric power.

To preserve the shoreline profile, some 30—50 per cent of shores suitable for recreational use may not be built on. Building is controlled to prevent the landscape from becoming spoiled.

Air pollution control and landscape conservation are fairly new activities in which good progress is being made. Closed seasons and other protective methods, nature protection areas, feeding of animals and other game management measures are applied to preserve threatened animal species.

Demographic Data

Finland's population in 1981 was 4,788,000. The country is rather sparsely populated with 15.6 inhabitants per sq. km. (Great Britain 228, USA 22). South and south-west Finland are the most densely populated parts; Lapland is thinly settled, having some districts with only 2—3 inhabitants per sq. km.

After 1880 the birth rate began to fall slowly, after 1910 rapidly. In 1931—35 it was 19.5 per 1,000 inhabitants (19.5 ‰) — roughly half of what it had been 50 years earlier. After the war there was a slight rise until 1958 when the birth rate fell to 18.5 per 1,000 inhabitants (1978 13.5 ‰). The death rate has fallen sharply since the end of the 19th century (1936—39 13—15 ‰; 1978 9.2 ‰).

Other recent statistics: Life expectancy, men 68.5 years, women 77.1 years — marriages per year 29,760 (6.3 ‰), — divorces per year 10,369 (2.18 ‰) — infant mortality 7.6 ‰ of live births (in 1938 67.8 ‰) — number of females per 1,000 males in towns 1,116, in rural areas 1,000 and in whole country 1,068.

Emigration

Emigration — especially to the USA and Canada — began as a mass movement in the 1880s, reaching its peak between 1901 and 1910, when 159,000 Finns emigrated. During World War I, the flow virtually ceased, but between 1921 and 1930 there were 58,600 emigrants. Inhabitants of Finnish origin in the USA in 1970 totalled around 203,800, approx. 45,500 of whom were born in Finland. The majority live in Michigan and Minnesota, where the climate and topography most resemble Finland. There are some 59,200 Finns in Canada and about 29,000 of them were born in Finland. Over half of the total live in Ontario. Since World War II, hundreds of thousands of Finns have left the country to settle abroad, approx. 300,000 of them in Sweden. Another recent trend has been emigration to Australia; the Finnish population there is around 15,000.

The biggest of Finland's 84 towns are: the capital Helsinki (483,700), Tampere (165,900), Turku (163,900), Espoo (133,700) and Vantaa (129,800). The smallest town is Kaskinen (1,900). This picture is of the centre of Helsinki.

Anthropological Characteristics

Finns are generally of light complexion, with fair hair and blue or grey eyes. 86 % of the Finnish-speaking men have blue or grey eyes, 81 % of the women. Fair or brown hair is found in 76 % of the men and 82 % of the women.

Racially the Finns are mixed, as are most European peoples. The main stocks apparently derive from the East Baltic and Nordic races.

The Finnish Language

Mikael Agricola (1510–1557), bishop, Finnish reformer, founder of Finnish literature and creator of the Finnish written language.

Finnish is not an Indo-European language, but together with Estonian, Hungarian and the languages of certain national minorities in Central and North Russia forms part of the Finno-Ugrian group (totalling 21–22 million people).

For centuries, the evolution of Finnish has been influenced by neighbouring Indo-European languages. In Finnish, however, loan words have changed less in the course of time than they have in their original languages. Thus the word *kuningas* is close to the earlier form of the English word "king".

Finnish, like Italian, is a euphonious language, with a wealth of vowels. Short or long vowels can occur in any syllable: *vaja,* for instance, is "shed", but *vaaja* means "wedge" and *vajaa* "scant". Diphthongs are also

11

common in Finnish; the language has relatively few consonants.

The orthography is simple, entirely phonetic. Pronunciation, too, is easy, the main stress invariably falling on the first syllable. Finnish is a highly inflected language, without articles or genders.

Other Languages

Finland has a Swedish-speaking minority. Part of this section of the population is descended from the Swedes who entered the country between the 9th and 13th centuries, and part is of Finnish ancestry who adopted Swedish when it was the language of the king and the educated.

In 1880, 14.3 % of the population still spoke Swedish as its mother tongue; by 1978 the proportion had fallen to 6.4 %, mainly due to a lower birth rate and a higher rate of emigration.

Although Finnish was established as a written language as early as the 16th century, Swedish remained the language of administration and culture until the latter part of the 19th century. In 1863, largely through the efforts of J.V. Snellman, Finnish was recognized as an official language on an equal footing with Swedish. According to the Government Act of 1919, Finnish and Swedish are the official languages of the Republic of Finland.

Lapp — also a Finno-Ugrian language — was spoken by 1,290 persons in Finnish Lapland in 1979.

There are around 200,000 reindeer in Finland. The animals are very important for the economy of the indigenous Lapps, who produce meat from the herds, but also use reindeer as draught animals. In the autumn, the reindeer are rounded up from the fells into corrals where the slaughter and draught reindeer are separated; the others are driven to the winter grazing grounds.

HISTORY

Bishop Henry, St. Henry, the Apostle of Finland". At his feet lies Lalli, the farmer who killed the bishop with an axe on frozen Lake Köyliönjärvi in 1156. From a mural in Taivassalo Church.

1155	The first Swedish crusade to Finland; Finland becomes part of the Kingdom of Sweden.
1809	Sweden surrenders Finland to Russia. Czar makes Finland an autonomous Grand Duchy.
1917	**Finnish declaration of independence,** Dec. 6, first recognized by Russia, France, Germany and Sweden.
1919	Present Constitution adopted; Finland becomes a Republic.

The first historical reference to the Finns is found in the "Germania" of Tacitus, the Roman historian. In fact, it was the Lapps, the country's earliest inhabitants, that he was describing. During the first century A.D. small groups of Finns began to migrate northwards to Finland from the Baltic countries. By about the year 1000, permanent settlements had developed and a national culture had been established, a culture that is reflected in the Finnish national epic, Kalevala. Christianity appeared in Finland in the course of the 11th century. In 1155 the Swedish King Erik the Good invaded Finland and secured the position of Christianity with the aid of the English-born Bishop Henry of Upsala. For 300 years, the Catholic Church had a dominating position in the country, but the Swedish government steadily consolidated its authority and by the time of the Reformation at the beginning of the 16th century had definitely established its power. The 16th century was, nevertheless, a period of strong national development, but progress was retarded during the next two centuries. From the middle of the 18th century the separatist movement grew stronger, fanned by the inability of Sweden to defend and further Finnish interests. Dissatisfaction culminated in the formation of the Anjala League against the King in 1788. As the result of the war of 1808—09, Sweden surrendered Finland to Russia. The country became an autonomous Grand Duchy, a union being created between Finland and Russia in the person of the Czar, who became Grand Duke of Finland. His powers in Finland were limited by the old Constitution which remained in force. Finland had its own Diet, government, administration, law and

courts, postal services, army (until 1904) and currency (from 1860). In 1906, the Diet of the Four Estates was replaced by a unicameral Parliament. In the same year, Finland was the first country in Europe to grant full political rights to women.

The growing force of Pan-Slavism in Russia swelled at the end of the century to take in Finland as well. Various attempts were made to russify Finland and the autonomous status of the country was violated. This provoked an attitude of passive resistance in Finland and a growing desire for complete independence. On December 6, 1917, after the October Revolution, Finland declared itself independent, but the effective start of political activity had to be postponed because of the outbreak of civil war. This was a struggle between the Red and White forces in Finland in which the Russian troops stationed in the country and a German expeditionary force participated. Peace was concluded with the Soviet Union in 1920. Relations between the two countries remained cool in the 1920s and 1930s. In 1938, the Soviet Union proposed certain security arrangements to Finland. When these talks failed, it demanded certain territorial concessions to improve the strategic position of Leningrad in October 1939. The ensuing negotiations ended in deadlock. The consequence was the Winter War of three and a half months, which ended with the cession of a part of south-east Finland to the Soviet Union. Following the outbreak of hostilities between Germany and the Soviet Union in 1941, Finland found itself engaged in the Continuation War with the Soviet Union. By the terms

The medieval castle of Turku was begun in the 1280s. The castle is now completely restored and contains a museum and the banquet and conference rooms of the City of Turku.

14

of the Armistice in September 1944, confirmed in Paris in 1947, Finland surrendered the territories it had occupied during the war and the Petsamo area which was its outlet to the Arctic Ocean.

In the light of the experience gained from these wars, the basic premiss adopted for Finnish foreign policy was that accession to anti-Soviet power groups would not be the historically correct solution to the Finnish security problem. That the primary interest of the Soviet Union in its north-west frontier is defensive by nature was taken as the basic hypothesis of the new foreign policy. If Finland were able by its foreign policy to guarantee that its territory would not be used for an offensive against the Soviet north-west frontier, this would cover the essential interest of the Soviet Union in Finnish territory and, at the same time, ensure the independence and territorial integrity of Finland.

Finland and the Soviet Union

Juho Kusti Paasikivi (1870–1956), banker, lawyer, diplomat, statesman. Prime Minister 1918, 1944–1946. President of the Republic 1946–1950 and 1950–1956. Creator of the "Paasikivi line", Finland's new foreign policy line after the wars, which has constituted the foundation for the development of friendly relations with the USSR.

Finnish-Soviet relations have developed favourably since the war. Both parties have striven to consolidate and advance the mutual confidence, respect and stability which characterize the actual state of relations between the two neighbouring countries. The Treaty of Friendship, Cooperation and Mutual Assistance, signed in 1948, was renewed in 1955 and 1970. This Treaty stands out as a basic document defining the relations between the two countries. The primary goal of the Soviet Union was to secure its north-western border with a treaty arrangement. The basic Finnish position was to gain more security for herself by recognizing the legitimacy of this defensive interest and also to obtain an agreement that would take into account Finland's desire to remain outside conflicts of interest between the great powers. The Treaty combines these two basic points of view and over the years it has retained its significance. Accordingly, Finnish-Soviet relations have not been affected by any fluctuations in international politics.

The relations between the two countries have been developed through various kinds of agreements. On the basis of an agreement on scientific and technical cooperation signed in 1955, Finland maintains specialized working groups in the fields of both fundamental research and applied sciences under the auspices of the joint committee specified in the agreement. An intergovernmental commission for economic cooperation has functioned since 1967. Its work has resulted in the institution of important joint projects, such as the current construction of the Kostamus mining and ore-dressing centre in Soviet Karelia, the enlargement of the Svetogorsk pulp mill

15

next to Imatra on the Soviet side, and copper smelting deliveries to the Norilsk plant in Siberia.

Finland imports natural gas from the Soviet Union through a pipeline constructed in the early seventies. Two of the four nuclear power plants in Finland have been built in technical and material cooperation with the Soviet Union. These plants, located in Lovisa on the southern coast, combine Soviet nuclear technology with Finnish and international safety standards. Finland's newest and largest steel mill, in Raahe, is largely a joint venture with the Soviet Union in technology as well as in part of the raw material supplies. Finns have constructed various hotels in Leningrad, Tallinn and Viborg, for example.

The commission for economic cooperation is charged with the exploration of joint projects on the territories of both parties. Its newest and most important function is, nevertheless, the follow-up of the long-term programme on developing and expanding cooperation in the fields of commerce, industry, science and technology. This programme was signed in 1977, and its term of validity has recently been extended until the end of 1995. The programme contains rather detailed and concrete recommendations in most fields of trade and industrial

The repeated personal contacts between President Urho Kekkonen and the Soviet Union's leaders have created an atmosphere of mutual understanding and trust between two states with different social orders.

cooperation. It is scheduled to cover two five-year periods over and above the current five year trade agreement. Such agreements on trade and payments have been in use since 1950 and coincide with the planning periods in the USSR. They are implemented through yearly protocols on the exchange of commodities.

Finland presently ranks second in the list of Soviet trading associates in the Western world. The Soviet Union is Finland's biggest single trade partner with a share of roughly one-fifth of Finland's foreign trade. Finland exports to the Soviet Union ships, forest industry machines, paper, consumer goods etc., and imports in return two-thirds of her crude oil, other energy products, industrial raw materials, machines etc.

One of the testimonies to the good development of Finnish-Soviet relations is the lease of a piece of Soviet territory to Finland. This is the Soviet sector of the Saimaa Canal, the waterway connecting Finnish inland waters with the Gulf of Finland and the Baltic. Transport facilities and tourism have been strongly developed between the two countries. Soviet tourists actually form the third largest group of foreign visitors to Finland.

Finland and Scandinavia

Finland has a close relationship with the other Nordic countries, Denmark, Iceland, Norway and Sweden. The main forum of cooperation between the five countries is the Nordic Council. It was established in 1952, and Finland joined it in 1955. The Council consists of 78 members elected by the five parliaments and the legislatures of the Faeroe Islands and Åland, and an unspecified number of Government representatives who are not entitled to vote. It cannot make decisions binding on member states, but its recommendations to Governments have led to several important measures of integration. A common labour market was established in 1954, granting citizens of member states the right to stay and work in any other Scandinavian countries without restrictions. A convention on social rights ensures that citizens of the five countries enjoy practically the same social benefits wherever they may reside in the Nordic area. No passports are required of citizens of member states for travel within the Nordic area. The Nordic countries also form a Passport Union in relation to the outside world. Citizens of one Nordic country residing in another Nordic country have been given the right to vote in municipal elections in their country of residence. The Nordic Council has also initiated steps to harmonise legislation in many fields, and its recommendations have led to the establishment of such joint research and educational institutions as the Scandinavian Institute of Theoretical Atomic Research and the Scandinavian College of Journalism in Denmark and the Nordic Art Centre in Finland.

Questions of foreign policy and defence remain outside the competence of the Nordic Council, but the foreign ministers of the five countries meet regularly twice a year to exchange views on matters of common interest, and at the United Nations the Scandinavian delegations form a recognized regional group. In 1962, the five countries passed an agreement on Nordic cooperation, the Helsinki Treaty. Its objective is to strengthen and expand the cooperation between the Nordic countries. As a result of a revision of the treaty in 1971 a joint Nordic Secretariat under the Presidium of the Nordic Council has been set up in Stockholm. Furthermore, a Nordic Council of Ministers with the whole field of Nordic cooperation as its area of activity has been created. The Nordic governments collaborate in this Council of Ministers and, as in the past, at informal Nordic Ministerial Meetings.

The decisions of the Council of Ministers, which must be unanimous, are binding on each Nordic Government. However, questions of major importance decided by the Council of Ministers are referred to the parliaments for final approval. Since 1973, the Council of Ministers has had a secretariat based in Oslo, while a joint Nordic Cultural Secretariat started operating in Copenhagen in 1972 as a result of a far-reaching Nordic Cultural Agreement between the five countries.

On the recommendation of the Nordic Council an agreement to establish a Nordic Investment Bank was signed in December 1975. The Bank's headquarters are in Helsinki. The object of the Bank is to promote investment and export undertakings of common Nordic interest by granting loans and giving bank guarantees. The Bank has an equity of 400 million SDRs and will seek to acquire additional funds from the international capital markets on favourable terms.

Finland and the United Nations

Although Finland annouced her interest in joining the United Nations as early as 1947, a membership dispute which was a reflection of the Cold War between the great powers prevented approval of Finland's application until 1955.

According to its charter the primary goal of the United Nations is to maintain and strengthen peace and international security. Finland, as a country pursuing a policy of neutrality and relying primarily on political

Finland has participated in the United Nations' peacekeeping operations since 1956 by sending troops and officers to serve in the UN forces. Lieutenant General Ensio Siilasvuo in Suez where on January 18, 1974, he witnessed the disengagement agreement between Egypt and Israel.

means for her security, has a vested interest in the creation of a more rational and peaceful world order. In its own work in the United Nations Finland has always stressed the importance of settling all disputes peacefully and has sought to make its own contribution to this end. President Kekkonen defined this position in an address before the General Assembly in 1961: We see ourselves as physicians rather than judges; it is not for us to pass judgement nor to condemn. It is rather to diagnose and to try to cure."

Finland has pursued an active policy in supporting the role of the United Nations as the main forum for disarmament, détente and development. In promoting these ideas Finland has been working closely with the other members of the Nordic groups, Denmark, Iceland, Norway and Sweden. These five countries, thanks to their joint and balanced stands, have gained considerable influence among the 154 member nations at the United Nations.

In the attempts to meet the just aspirations of the developing countries, Finland has supported the goals of the New International Economic Order. Finland has accordingly participated actively in the ongoing dialogue between the North and the South as progress in this field is of paramount importance not only to the developing countries but also with regard to the interests of the entire world community.

Also within the UN Finland has stressed the importance of safeguarding human rights, and has, for example, taken a strong stand against South Africa's policy of apartheid. Finland has also played a major role in UN efforts to establish an independent Namibia, and thereby end South Africa's illegal rule there.

Of special importance has been the Finnish contribution to UN peace-keeping forces. In proportion to its population, Finland is the leading contributor to these forces. Approximately 16,500 Finnish soldiers have served under the UN flag, and the Finnish contingents have accounted for 7 to 30 per cent of the troops in the various peacekeeping operations. Thanks to the policy of neutrality it pursues, Finland has been among the small number of countries which have been acceptable to both sides in various disputes. The role of peacekeeping troops in the Middle East and Cyprus has also been of global significance.

Since the end of the 1960s increased Finnish activity in the United Nations has been evident in e.g. expanding representation in the various UN organs. The most important examples are Finland's participation in the Security Council in 1969–70 and in the Economic and Social Council in 1972–74 and 1978–80. Finns have served at the UN in many high positions under the

High-ranking participants in the closing session of the Conference on Security and Cooperation in Europe in Helsinki in 1975: Urho Kekkonen, President of Finland, Valery Giscard d'Estaing, President of France, and Harold Wilson, Prime Minister of Great Britain.

inlande   France   Grand

ésident

Secretary-General. Currently, ambassador Martti
Ahtisaari is the UN Commissioner for Namibia, Klaus
Sahlgren is the executive director of the UN Centre on
Transnational Corporations, and Major General Erkki
Kaira is the commander of the UN disengagement
observer force in the Golan Heights.

Finnish Foreign Policy

Finland has long sought security by remaining outside
international conflicts and entanglements. It continues
to do so and has hitherto been successful. Its security
does not rest on military alliances or on the protection
offered by one power bloc pitted against another.
Instead, neutrality and friendly relations with all
countries, especially its neighbours, built on mutual
confidence are the basis of Finnish foreign policy. Still,
neutrality does not mean isolation; promoting the
peaceful settlement of conflicts and developing
international cooperation are integral parts of Finnish
policy.

Using this approach, Finland has consolidated its
position in European affairs and its policy of neutrality
has won wide international recognition. Perhaps the best
indications of the confidence and respect this policy
enjoys are the assignments entrusted to Finland during
the past decade. In 1969—72 Finland, together with
Austria, hosted the Strategic Arms Limitation Talks
between the United States and the Soviet Union. At the
same time Finland also worked to promote European
security.

Negotiations started on Finland's initiative and carried
out from 1969 to 1972 led to the commencement of the
historically significant Conference on Security and
Cooperation in Europe in Helsinki on July 3, 1973. This
first stage approved recommendations for the
committee stage which was held in Geneva from
mid-September 1973 to mid-July 1975.

The third stage of the conference was held in Helsinki
from July 30 to August 1, 1975, on the highest political
level. The Final Act of the CSCE was signed at the end
of the conference. The Act is a political document whose
significance is underlined by the fact that it was signed
by the highest political leaders of the 35 participating
states.

Finland participated actively also in the first follow-up
conference, held in Belgrade from November 4, 1977 to
March 8, 1978. At this conference a decision was made
to continue the implementation of the provisions of the
Final Act and ensure the continuation of the CSCE
process by agreeing to hold the next follow-up
conference in Madrid, as well as three meetings of

experts. The expert meetings were held in Bonn ("Scientific Forum", 1978), Montreaux (peaceful solution of disputes, 1978) and Valletta (cooperation in the Mediterranean, 1979). The follow-up meeting in Madrid started in November 1980.

In recent years Finland has taken a keen interest in arms control and disarmament. As a small, neutral country Finland believes that progress in disarmament will strengthen its own security and contribute to the general process of détente.

In addition to acting as a host to important disarmament negotiations between the United States and the Soviet Union, Finland has been especially active in the fields of non-proliferation of nuclear weapons and nuclear-weapon-free zones, and has participated in the work of controlling chemical weapons and in seismological monitoring of a comprehensive test ban.

Finland made a proposal concerning a nuclear-weapon-free zone in the Nordic region as early as 1963. This proposal was further developed in 1978 and has lately been the subject of a lively discussion.

Trade and Economic Relations with the Outside World

Finland's economy, like that of many other industrialized countries with a high standard of living, is largely dependent on foreign trade. Exports of goods and services are running at 27 % of the GNP. Economic growth has been rapid in the last two decades. Including the years of global recession in the 1970's, the GNP increased at an average annual rate of 3 % during 1973–80 and the volume of exports at a rate of 5 %. Exports have at the same time been considerably diversified.

Finland has constantly aimed at developing trade with all countries on a liberal and non-discriminatory basis. Naturally, Europe accounts for the bulk of our foreign trade; the Soviet Union, Sweden, the Federal Republic of Germany and Great Britain are the leading individual trading partners. Outside Europe the main trading partners are the United States, the OPEC countries and Japan. The share of market economy countries in Finnish foreign trade is roughly four-fifths and that of the socialist countries one-fifth. Trade and economic relations are based on a large number of multilateral and bilateral agreements.

Western Europe accounts for roughly two-thirds of Finland's foreign trade. The move towards economic integration, which started with the creation of the European Economic Community (EEC) and the European Free Trade Association (EFTA), led Finland to seek appropriate solutions to safeguard its commercial interests and competitive position in these important markets. In 1961 Finland became an associate member of EFTA under the FINEFTA agreement. The agreement provided for the gradual elimination of tariffs and other barriers to trade between Finland and the seven EFTA member countries. The goals were reached in 1967, and trade under these arrangements has developed favourably.

In the beginning of the 1970's new constellations emerged in the European market. The United Kingdom and Denmark decided to withdraw from EFTA and join the EEC in 1973. Although they preserved EFTA, the remaining EFTA countries, including Finland, initiated negotiations on free trade agreements with the enlarged Community in 1971. At the end of 1973, Finland concluded its negotiations and signed bilateral agreements with the EEC and the European Coal and Steel Community. According to these agreements, duty-free trade in industrial goods was implemented gradually by July 1, 1977, except for a number of sensitive products for which there is a transition period up to 1985.

In the field of East-West economic relations Finland is a pioneer. Finland has long-standing and advanced economic relations with the Soviet Union. Soviet trade currently accounts for about one-fifth of Finland's total trade. The 1960 tariff agreement with the USSR ensures for that country the same tariff benefits as those accorded the EFTA countries under the FINEFTA agreement, and the same provision was made when Finland signed its agreement with the EEC on free trade in industrial goods. Finland has also concluded agreements on the reciprocal dismantling of barriers to trade with Bulgaria, Hungary, Czechoslovakia, the GDR and Poland. Finnish agreements on technological and industrial cooperation with the socialist countries have opened up new vistas, especially in exchanges with the Soviet Union. Finland was the first market economy country to make an agreement (in 1973) on economic cooperation with the Council for Mutual Economic Assistance (Comecon).

In a wider framework, Finland has taken part in the work of the General Agreement on Tariffs and Trade (GATT) since 1949 and has participated actively in the negotiation rounds on the elimination of tariffs and other barriers to trade. With the exception of some agricultural products, imports are not subject to quantitative restrictions, and the average tariff on dutiable goods is less than 12 %. Finland is a member of the Organization for Economic Cooperation and Development (OECD).

Trade with developing countries deserves increasing attention. In 1972 Finland introduced the so-called Generalized System of Preferences, which provides for the duty-free entry of manufactured goods, semi-manufactures, raw materials and tropical products from these countries. More than 100 developing countries now benefit from this system, which was created by the United Nations Conference on Trade and Development (UNCTAD).

THE STATE

Kaarlo Juho Ståhlberg (1865–1952), lawyer, statesman. The first President of the Republic, 1919–1925. An authority on Finnish constitutional and administrative law.

Finland is a sovereign republic. The Parliament Act was passed in 1906 (amended 1928), and the Government Act was adopted in 1919. Legislative power is vested in Parliament acting in conjunction with the President. The supreme executive power is vested in the President, who makes his decisions in Cabinet meetings on the basis of the recommendation of the Government minister responsible for the matter. Judicial power rests with independent courts of justice.

The President is elected for a term of 6 years by an Electoral College of 301 that is returned in the same way as Parliament. He can veto a bill passed by Parliament by withholding his signature. But if Parliament after a general election then passes it again without amendment, it automatically becomes law. The President can issue statutes and decrees which do not amend existing law. He is Commander-in-Chief of the Defence Forces, but in case of war may delegate his authority. He is responsible for Finland's relations with foreign powers, but decisions of war and peace and more important treaties must be approved by Parliament.

The 200 members of the unicameral Parliament are elected every four years by equal and universal suffrage. The voting age is 18 and the system is proportional representation. Every voter, with a few exceptions, is entitled to stand for election.

The Cabinet, presided over by the Prime Minister, is responsible for the general conduct of administrative affairs. It must enjoy the confidence of Parliament. Its members are appointed by the President. The President also appoints the Chancellor of Justice, who attends Cabinet sessions, particularly those presided over by the President. He has no veto or voting power, but gives authoritative advice on the legality of the Government's actions. His tenure of office does not end with a change of Government. His office is approximately equivalent to that of the Attorney General in Britain. He is assisted and supported by the Ombudsman to Parliament who is elected by Parliament for four years at a time, and might be likened to the Solicitor General in the British parliamentary system.

The practical work of administration is done by various government organs and officials. Some administrative functions are delegated to self-governing bodies, such as local government authorities and the Church.

The rights and obligations of citizens are laid down in the Constitution. The most important rights are equality before the law, security of life, liberty and property, protection of labour, freedom of worship, speech, publication, meeting and association. The obligations include compulsory military service for men.

```
┌─────────────── Presidents of the Republic ───────────────┐
│                                                           │
│      1919−1925    K.J. Ståhlberg                          │
│      1925−1931    Lauri Kr. Relander                      │
│      1931−1937    P.E. Svinhufvud                         │
│      1937−1940    Kyösti Kallio                           │
│      1940−1943    Risto Ryti                              │
│      1943−1944    Risto Ryti                              │
│      1944−1946    G. Mannerheim                           │
│      1946−1950    J.K. Paasikivi                          │
│      1950−1956    J.K. Paasikivi                          │
│      1956−1962    U.K. Kekkonen                           │
│      1962−1968    U.K. Kekkonen                           │
│      1968−1974    U.K. Kekkonen                           │
│      1974−1978    U.K. Kekkonen                           │
│      1978−1982    U.K. Kekkonen                           │
│                                                           │
└───────────────────────────────────────────────────────────┘
```

Representation in Parliament

	1966	1970	1972	1975	1979
Finnish People's Democratic League	41	36	37	40	35
Finnish Social Democratic Party	55	52	55	54	52
Centre Party	50	36	35	39	36
Liberal People's Party	8	8	7	9	4
Finnish Christian League	−	1	4	9	9
National Coalition Party	26	37	34	35	47
Finnish Rural Party	1	18	18	2	7
Swedish People's Party	12	12	10	10	10
Other parties	7	−	−	2	−

The Political Parties

Eight parties are represented in Parliament. They are, in order of size: the Finnish Social Democratic Party (f. 1899, roughly equivalent to the British Labour Party), the National Coalition Party (f. 1918, conservative), the Centre Party (f. 1906, formerly the Agrarian Union; represents chiefly the rural population and the political centre), the Finnish People's Democratic League (f. 1944, represents socialists and communists), the Swedish People's Party (f. 1906, represents mainly the interests of the Swedish-speaking minority), the Finnish Christian League (f. 1958, bases its policy on the

Facade of the Parliament Building. Architect: J.S. Sirén, 1927—31.

Christian faith), the Finnish Rural Party (f. 1959, split off from the Centre Party; represents chiefly the small farmers) and the Liberal People's Party (f. 1965, liberal reform party, represents the political centre).

A feature of the multi-party system is that the balance of political power does not change much from one parliamentary election to another.

Largely because of the proportional representation system, no party has held an absolute majority in Parliament during the period of independence. Most governments have been coalition or minority cabinets.

Administration

The Cabinet, presided over by the Prime Minister, is responsible for the general administration of the country. There are 11 ministries, viz. for Foreign Affairs, Justice, Interior Affairs, Defence, Finance, Education, Agriculture and Forestry, Transport and Communications, Labour, Trade and Industry, Health and Social Welfare. Some of the ministries have two ministers. Subordinated to the ministries are central boards which delegate matters to local authorities.

For administrative purposes the country is divided into provinces and municipalities. There are 12 provinces, each controlled by a provincial government headed by a Governor. The State is responsible for the administration of the provinces, while that of the municipalities is based on local self-government. One of the provinces, the Åland Islands, enjoys a special autonomous position so as to preserve its Swedish-language culture.

There are 464 municipalities in Finland, 84 with the status of towns (i.e. cities).

The municipalities collect their own taxes, manage their own economic affairs, maintain public order and

27

attend to all matters not specifically delegated by law to other authorities. Decisions are made by municipal councils elected by proportional representation for terms of 4 years. Executive and administrative authority is generally entrusted to municipal boards and officials. The day-to-day running of municipal affairs is usually entrusted to salaried local government officials. These include a Town Director and Town Secretary in urban districts and corresponding officials in other municipalities.

Municipalities are free to collaborate among themselves and set up inter-municipal corporations for the maintenance of public institutions and the management of other undertakings.

The Judicial System

Justice is administered in Finland by independent courts.

The public Courts of Justice try both civil and criminal cases. In rural areas, courts of the first instance are known as Circuit Courts, the judicial authority reposing in a legally trained judge and a jury of between five and twelve lay members. The circuits are divided into assizes, which meet at regular intervals and have their own jurors. The jury can, by unanimous decision, override the judge. In the towns, the courts of the first instance are the Town Courts, each presided over by a legally trained magistrate and two Counsellors. Courts of the second instance are the six Courts of Appeal, each with a President, sometimes a Vice-President, and a number of Counsellors of Appeal. These courts hear appeals from lower courts and in certain criminal cases act as courts of the first instance. The highest juridical authority rests with the Supreme Court, to which appeals may be made against the judgments of the Courts of Appeal. The right to appeal is subject to certain limitations. The Supreme Court is composed of a President and a number of Counsellors of Justice. In lower courts cases are dealt with orally and later documented, but in higher courts mostly in writing.

There is also an extraordinary tribunal known as the High Court of Impeachment. This is convoked when necessary and deals with the impeachment of Cabinet members and other high government officials.

Litigation in administrative matters is handled in lower instances by government officials. In higher instances it becomes a matter for the Supreme Administrative Court, composed of a President and a number of Administrative Counsellors. The Civil Service High Court handles disciplinary cases against civil servants, the Ministry of Justice matters of judicial administration.

The Prisons Department of the Ministry of Justice

administers Finland's prisons: 4 central prisons, 1 central and provincial prison, 1 prison for young offenders, 7 provincial prisons and 4 reserve prisons.

Police

The highest direction and control of the police comes under the Ministry of the Interior, which has a special Police Division for the purpose. The head of the division is the supreme head of the police. In each province the police force is controlled and directed by the Provincial Government, which has a special police office for the purpose. The local police forces of a province are divided into police districts, headed by chiefs of police. The urban police forces are headed by a police commissioner.

The Central Criminal Police, the Mobile Police and the Security Police are under the direct supervision of the Ministry of the Interior. Finland is a member of Interpol.

The Finnish Defence Forces

Gustaf Mannerheim (1867–1951), Baron, Marshal of Finland. Served in Russian Army 1887–1917. Returned to Finland in 1917. Regent of Finland 1918–19. Commander-in-Chief of Finnish armed forces in the Winter War of 1939–40 and the war of 1941–44. President of the Republic, 1944–46.

The duties of the Defence Forces were stated in law in 1974. According to this law the Defence Forces are to
– be responsible for the surveillance of the nation's land and sea territories and its air space in cooperation with other surveillance authorities,
– secure the territorial integrity of the nation, if necessary by resorting to force,
– defend the nation and its legal system and the security of its people,
– be in charge of the maintenance and development of the nation's military defensive preparedness,
– give military training and take part in promoting the willingness to defend the country and improving the physical fitness of the population,
– assist in the establishment of United Nations peacekeeping forces.

Military defence is primarily a factor preventing the nation from getting involved in war. Thus the duties of the Defence Forces are in line with the basic aims of the nation's security policy.

According to the law on universal conscription every male citizen from the age of 17 to 60 is liable to military service. Annually about 93 % of the age group are found fit for military service at incall examinations. Roughly 40,000 men receive military training every year.

During their period of military service men, at the age of 20, are instructed in the basic duties of a soldier. The period of service for those drafted to reserve officer or non-commissioned officer training or certain special duties is eleven months, while the ordinary conscript serves eight months. Conscripts enter the Army and the Air Force three times a year. Those who are drafted into the Navy commence their service in two contingents.

The reserve forces are given complementary training on refresher courses which are annually attended by 35,000 reservists. The trained and equipped reserves comprise roughly 700,000 men.

The military defence is based on a territorial defence system according to which the country is divided into seven military areas. The idea is to take advantage of the circumstances which are peculiar to the territory and weather conditions of Finland.

The equipment of the Defence Forces is to a large extent of domestic manufacture. Finnish industry has produced the assault rifles which are used by every soldier, anti-tank weapons, transport equipment and gunboats and mine-sweepers used by the Navy. The Army radio equipment and part of the material of the field artillery is Finnish-built, as is the radar equipment for low surveillance.

The Air Force's most important combat aircraft are Soviet Migs and Swedish Drakens. The latter are assembled by Valmet Oy in Finland.

Finland has participated in United Nations peacekeeping operations since 1956. Finnish soldiers have occupied the posts of military adviser, military observer and commander, and Finnish contingents have been at the disposal of the United Nations at Sinai, Suez, Cyprus and the Golan Heights. In 1981 a Finnish battalion of 390 men was serving in the Golan Heights between Israel and Syria, and Finland had eleven men serving in Cyprus, 21 military observers in the Middle East and four in Kashmir. Altogether more than 6,500 Finnish soldiers have participated in United Nations peacekeeping operations.

One of the Finnish navy's newest vessels is the mine layer Pohjanmaa, which was built by the Wärtsilä Helsinki Shipyard in 1979. The ship has a length of 78 metres and a beam of 11.5 metres. The two Finnish-made diesel engines have a combined output of 4,300 kW and give the ship a speed of about 20 knots. The Pohjanmaa has a displacement of 1,100 tons.

The Church

Since 1923, there has been complete freedom of worship in Finland. Every citizen is at liberty to adopt any religious faith he pleases, or none.

In 1978, 90.6 % of the population belonged to the Evangelical Lutheran Church of Finland, 1.2 % to the Orthodox Church of Finland, 0.1 % to the Roman Catholic Church and 8.1 % to other religious groups or no church.

The Evangelical Lutheran Church

The Evangelical Lutheran Church is self-governing, with government control over certain matters only.

The Church Assembly is the highest organ of church self-government and meets twice a year. Its members comprise 64 laymen and 32 clergymen, all elected. The bishops, and the representatives of the Government, the Supreme Court and the Supreme Administrative Court are members by virtue of office. In its capacity as a decision-making body the Church Assembly makes proposals to Parliament for amendments to the Church Act. Parliament can either approve or reject these, but not alter them. The Church Assembly is also responsible for the church's Central Treasury, through which wealthy parishes subsidize those in a weak financial position. The Ecclesiastical Board, chaired by the Archbishop, prepares matters for the Church Assembly and sees to it that its decisions are carried out.

The country is divided into 8 dioceses, each with a Bishop and Chapter. One of these dioceses is administered in Swedish. Bishops are appointed by the President of the Republic on the basis of elections held by the clergy of each diocese. Since 1817, the Bishop of Turku has held the rank of Archbishop. The dioceses are divided into deaneries (76 in 1978) which are sub-divided into parishes (593). The parishes are independent as regards internal affairs. They have the right to collect taxes from all members of the Church and from corporations and other organizations. They elect their own clergy.

The Orthodox Church

The Orthodox Church of Finland owes allegiance to the Ecumenical Patriarch of Constantinople. The highest administrative authority is vested in the Government, religious matters being determined by the Bishop's Conference and Church Assembly. General administration lies with the Bishops and the Central Board of the Church. The Church is divided into 3 dioceses, Karelia, Helsinki and Oulu, and 25 parishes. The present Bishop of Karelia is the Archbishop. The Orthodox Church has one monastery and one nunnery.

THE ECONOMY

General

Up to the middle of the 19th century farming, supplemented by fishing and hunting, was the main source of livelihood for an overwhelming majority of the population. The process of industrialization did not really gain momentum until the 1860s. At the outbreak of World War II it had made considerable progress and Finland's great forest resources had achieved the dominant position they still hold in the national economy.

In 1917, when Finland became an independent republic and the ties with the old Russian Empire were broken, new opportunities for foreign trade opened and the 20 years between the two World Wars were a period of lively economic progress. In Finland, as elsewhere, the depression of the early 1930s interrupted this favourable trend, but it was surmounted sooner than in many other countries. The late thirties was a period of increasing prosperity. Finland established itself as one of the world's leading producers and exporters of wood and paper products. Despite its limited mineral resources and complete lack of indigenous solid and liquid fuels (wood and peat excepted), other sectors of industry, especially the metal and engineering industry made considerable progress. Agriculture was modernized and intensified, and on the eve of World War II Finland was practically self-supporting in cereal crops and was exporting considerable quantities of dairy produce.

Although material damage was less severe in Finland than in many other countries, the economy suffered considerably from the war. The cost of peace was also heavy. Finland lost one-tenth of its productive capacity and resources; over 400,000 people had to leave their homes and, in many cases, to change their occupations; the country had to pay war reparations out of a diminished national income. Nevertheless, the post-war recovery was faster than most Finns had anticipated.

The economy is based on the principles of private ownership and free enterprise. In certain sectors the State has a de jure (production and sale of alcohol) or de facto (e.g. the railways) monopoly. In most branches, however, the State owns only one of the many firms. It is the largest forest owner in the country, controlling 28.5 % of the total forest area; of the arable land it owns less than 1 %.

The period of autumnal russeting", a brief week or so, is the most fascinating seasonal change in Lapland: entire fell slopes flame with the yellow of the birches, in the uplands the bog bilberries glow violet and the blackberry takes on every shade of red. The red whortleberry and the crowberry retain their summery green. The blue of the limpid ponds sets the seal on this feast of colour.

The Finnish year is sharply divided into the 4 seasons — winter, spring, summer and autumn. Southern Finland is covered in snow for an average of 5 months, and in February, the coldest month, the average temperature is −6 ° to −12 °C.

*South Karelia, in south-east Finland, is
hilly and varied: dense forests, barren
forest land, limpid lakes. The fields are
undulating and small in size, often very
stony. The stones have been gathered in
the course of time into mounds or used to
build partitioning walls. This is
Savitaipale, close to Lappeenranta.*

Folk music has enjoyed an unprecedented period of popularity in recent years. The explanation is to be found in the international folk music festival at Kaustinen, Central Ostrobothnia, a highlight of the lively cultural activities of the summer. Close on a thousand performers — fiddlers, groups of dancers and singers from Finland and overseas — meet. Tens of thousands come to watch and hear. The picture shows a group from Kaustinen with Konsta Jylhä, the most highly regarded performer and composer of Finnish folk music, as the soloist.

The golden era of the Finnish ryijy» runs from the middle of the 18th century to the early 19th century. Wandering professional weavers did the work. The colour scheme was based on domestic vegetable dyes, the pattern design was free, no precise drawings were used. This one is from Nummi, province of Uusimaa, 1805.

The Finnish art nouveau of the beginning of the century had a stamp of its own; it stuck to a national basis. Selim Lindqvist (1867–1939) combined neo-Gothic features with the form language of the art nouveau in his works. The entrance hall of a private house, Villa Johanna, designed by him (Helsinki, 1905–1906).

Pekka Halonen (1865–1933) is a lyrical depicter of light and harmonious Finnish scenery.   An autumnal willow" (1907).

*Finland is traditionally a major exporter
of paper and pulp. It also exports
woodworking and paper machinery and
even complete plants. The picture shows
Enso-Gutzeit's sulphate pulp mill in
Kaukopää, the largest of its kind in Europe.*

The Finnish shipbuilding industry maintains high standards and is extensively specialized: luxury cruise liners, oil-drilling rigs and icebreakers which are among the most effective in the world. The Urho class icebreaker has yet to be defeated by ice: in tests it broke a wall of pack ice over 20 m thick.

Arabia's Ruska dishes have been conquering the world for 20 years: a living surface and individual glazing are combined with the rustic stoneware. Ruska is oven-proof and tolerates machine washing. The picture also shows new enamelware by Arabia.

Vuokko dresses have clear lines and pure colours. The material is natural fibre. Design: Vuokko Eskolin-Nurmesniemi.

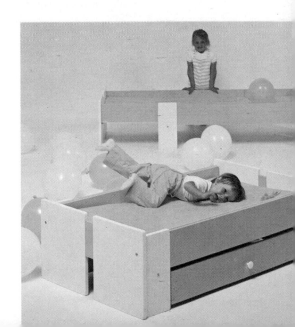

Muurame Oy's collection, designed by Pirkko Stenros, consists of solid, well functioning modular chests, shelves and beds, many of which are specially made for children.

Together with the size of the Peony plate
the flower grows from bud to full bloom.
A free-formed rim, which suits the rustic,
hand-made Peony style frames the
flower. Designed by Oiva Toikka. Peony is
accompanied by Viapori glass, designed by
Inkeri Toikka. Arabia glass collection
from Wärtsilä, Nuutajärvi Glass.

*Kalevala ornaments are copies of old
Finnish jewellery, the earliest of which
dates from the 5th century. The materials
are gold, silver and bronze. The artists of
Kalevala Koru also design modern
costume jewellery and often use Finnish
species of precious stones in them.*

The Empire style centre of Helsinki. In
the foreground is the market place, the most
popular shopping and strolling place in
the capital, in the centre is the Town Hall,
and behind it stands the Cathedral.

May 1st is the traditional spring
festival of students, workers and children.
The Esplanade in Helsinki.

Olavinlinna Castle, built in the 15th century, is one of the most imposing of Finland's medieval castles. It is the scene every summer of the great Savonlinna Opera Festival.

Economic Situation

Finland, like all the other countries of Western Europe, suffered its worst recession since the Second World War in the mid 70s. The slump started in Finland in 1975, later than in most industrial countries. In 1978, for the fourth consecutive year, economic growth remained around zero. In 1979 and 1980, however, Finland's economic growth was among the highest in the OECD at 7 and 6 per cent.

Unemployment is still the economy's most serious problem even after two years of fast growth. Since 1975 a number of other important economic problems have also caused the government concern:

1. The first energy crisis led to an immediate rise in the price of energy imports and consequently an 8 billion mark deficit in the balance of payments for 1975. The deficit was 8 per cent of the gross national product and one-third of the value of total exports. It was of course possible to finance the deficit through short- and long-term capital imports, but this led to a doubling of the foreign debt. In 1976 Finland's foreign debt totalled 25 billion marks. The recovery of exports and decreases in imports as a result of negative income growth have quickly balanced the current account.

2. Inflationary pressures originally due to foreign trade factors were aggravated by excessive wage and salary increases negotiated by Finland's labour market organizations. Consequently, prices rose by 7, 10, 16, 18, 14 and 13 per cent a year beginning in 1972 (using the consumer price index as the standard). In 1978 inflation finally returned to 7 per cent. The acceleration of economic growth nevertheless restored double-digit inflation: consumer prices rose 8 per cent in 1979 and 12 per cent in 1980.

3. In 1974 less than 2 per cent of the labour force was unemployed, but with the growth of demand shrinking to zero for the second, third and fourth time in 1976–78, unemployment reached record proportions: 85,000 (3.9 per cent) in 1976, 137,000 (6.4 per cent) in 1977 and 169,000 (7,9 per cent) in 1978. When the recession began to let up, the jobless figures also started decreasing: in 1979 there were 137,000 jobless (6.2 per cent of the labour force) and in 1980 there were 115,000 (5.1 per cent).

In 1978 Finland's gross national product per capita, $6,820, put the country 21st in the world. Finland was behind such nations as West Germany, France and all the Scandinavian countries, while it outranked England, New Zeeland, Israel and all the socialist countries. Finland's annual growth figure of 5.2 per cent for 1965–74 was higher than that of any of the countries mentioned.

Gross National Product in 1979

at factor cost

	Million Fmk	%
Agriculture	6,191	4
Forestry and fishing	7,198	5
Manufacturing	46,699	32
Construction	10,478	7
Trade, restaurants and hotels	16,307	11
Transport and communication	12,375	9
Banking and insurance	5,145	4
Ownership of dwellings	10,217	7
Other services	29,808	21
Total	144,418	100

In 1978, the gross national product per capita was the equivalent of US $6,820. The corresponding figures for some other countries were: Sweden $10,210, USA $9,700, Federal Republic of Germany $9,600, Canada $9,170, Australia $7,920, Japan $7,330 and Great Britain $5,030.

The Monetary System

Finland's monetary system is under the control of Suomen Pankki (the Bank of Finland), a bank of issue established in 1811 and supervised by Parliament. The monetary unit is the markka (Finnmark, 1 markka = 100 pennies). The last par value of the mark was set on October 12, 1967, and was 0.21159 grams of fine gold per mark (equivalent, at the time, to 4.20 marks per US dollar). Since November 1, 1977, the external value of the mark has been officially expressed in terms of a currency index. This index is trade-weighted and indicates the average change in the currencies which are important in Finnish foreign trade. On September 1, 1981, the selling rate of the Bank of Finland was Fmk 4.556 and the buying rate Fmk 4.538 per US dollar.

The regulations for the Bank of Finland limit the notes in circulation to a maximum of Fmk 700 million over the Bank's total gold reserves and proved foreign balances.

Public Finance

The public sector is divided in Finland into general government and local government (municipalities and inter-municipal corporations). The aim is not to achieve a profit, but to moderate economic inequality and to produce collective commodities. Revenue consists chiefly of taxes. The share of both indirect and direct taxes in total revenue has grown steadily; in direct

Johan Vilhelm Snellman, (1806–1881) philosopher, social writer, journalist, one of Finland's most notable statesmen, a national leader. He also established the monetary system of Finland.

taxation the emphasis is shifting from corporate bodies to households.

The wage-earner pays income tax (progressive) on his earnings to the State and municipal tax (proportional) to his municipality of domicile. The tax payable on income and property is assessed in accordance with scales that are fixed yearly. All taxes and the national pension and health insurance contribution may be at the most 80 % of the taxable income.

Corporate taxation is based on what is called the income and expenditure theory. Farming is taxed on the basis of pure income and forestry on the basis of area. Other forms of taxation are turnover tax, motor vehicle tax, excise taxes, stamp duty and alcohol taxes.

Public finance has been swollen greatly by e.g. the growth of public health care and education and the increase in income transfers under the social security system.

Public Finance

State revenue and expenditure in 1979 and 1980 (million Fmk)

Revenue	1979	1980
Income & wealth tax	9,471	12,213
Sales tax	10,649	12,262
Custom duties & import charges	1,103	1,381
Excise duties	5,715	6,487
Revenue from the Alcohol Monopoly	2,489	2,746
Other taxes & income of a tax-like nature	4,244	4,295
Taxes & duties total	33,671	39,384
Interests, dividends, etc.	1,014	1,056
Other revenue	2,716	3,110
Redemptions of loans granted	750	751
A. Revenue excl. state borrowing	38,151	44,301
Expenditure	1979	1980
Wages, salaries, pensions	7,033	7,954
Other consumption expenditure	4,788	5,749
State subsidies & transfer expenditure	22,759	25,485
Real investments	3,944	4,098
Lending & other financial investments	3,469	3,889
Interest, index compensations & other exp.	825	1,262

B. Expenditure excl. redemptions	42,818	48,437
A−B.	−4,667	−4,136
State borrowing		
Foreign	2,559	1,791
Domestic	2,184	3,211
Redemptions		
Foreign	275	269
Domestic	907	1,234
C. Long-term borrowing, net	+3,561	+3,499
A−B+C	−1,106	−637

Agriculture

Agriculture employs about 12 % of the population but its share of the GNP is only approx. 4 %. Finnish agriculture is characterized by small family farms averaging 11 ha of arable land and 35 ha of forest. Farmers receive 43 % of their income from milk production, 29 % from meat and 13 % from sales of grain. Forestry provides an important source of additional income through timber sales and logging work.

Crops such as wheat, rye, barley, oats, potatoes, sugar-beet and vegetables reach their northern limits in Finland. Their production is sufficient to satisfy domestic consumption, except for sugar, of which approx. 50 % is imported. Finland is over 100 % self-sufficient in dairy husbandry and a net exporter of dairy products.

Output, Net Imports (+) and Net Exports (−) of Some Agricultural Products (mill. kg)

Wheat	Rye	Barley	Oats	Potatoes	Butter	Cheese	Beef	Pork	Eggs
357	124	1,534	1,258	736	74	73	114	169	79
296	−	−	−	−	−10	−41	−	−15	−26

Fishing and Hunting

Fishing, unlike hunting, has survived as an important source of food production. There are some 7,500 commercial fishermen, 2,100 of whom derive their livelihood entirely from fishing. Baltic herring is the most important marine species, followed by pike, salmon, sea trout and whitefish. Over 70 million kg of Baltic herring is caught yearly; the catch of all other fish is considerably less than 20 million kg.

Finland no longer has any commercial hunters, but

A "new generation tractor", the Valmet 1502, went into production in 1976. Manoeuvrability and safety are salient features in its design. The surface pressure is small because the chassis consists of a bogie with two traction wheels on each side, instead of large traction rear wheels. Equipped with tracks the unit can work in swamps, difficult snow conditions and soft forest terrain.

ptarmigan is of considerable importance for the local inhabitants in North Finland. The number who hunt for sport is increasing and already stands at approx. 270,000, which is high in relation to the total population. An average of 60,000 elk are, for instance, shot yearly.

Forestry

The primary importance of the forest for the national economy of Finland is readily understandable from the fact that the forests are the country's principal natural resource. They cover 65 % of the land area. After the Soviet Union and Sweden, Finland has the third largest forest area in Europe — over 19.7 million ha. There are thus about 4 ha of forest land per inhabitant. The total growing stock of the forests is 1,520 million solid cu.m. (incl. bark) and the annual increment is 57 million solid cu.m. (incl. bark). The main tree species are pine (45 % of the growing stock), spruce (37 %), birch (15 %) and aspen and alder (3 %). The long and strong fibre of the first two of these is in particular demand in the pulp industry, the largest timber consuming branch in the Finnish forest industry. Larger sizes of the slow-growing coniferous timber are used in the sawmill industry. The principal form of utilization for birch is plywood manufacture, but increasing amounts of smaller-sized birch are also used by the chemical pulp industry. The consumption of wood has increased with the fast growth in the production capacity of the forest industry. The amount of roundwood used by the industry in 1980 was 48 million cu.m.

A large-scale improvement programme for silviculture and soil improvement has been in the process of implementation since the 1960s. Its aims are to replace slow-growing and poorly productive forests, to drain swamps for afforestation and to fertilize the forests. If the programme is completed as planned, the annual cut can be increased by between 7 and 17 million cu.m. (incl. bark) by the year 2000, depending on the scope of the improvements.

Finnish forests are to a great extent (65 %) in the hands of private owners, generally farmers, who depend upon forestry for an essential part of their income. Many of the smaller farmers work in the forests in winter. Thus forestry is of decisive importance to the rural population.

Forest land: 19.7 mill. ha
Growing stock: 1,520 mill. solid cu.m. incl. bark
Annual increment 57.4 mill. solid cu.m. incl. bark
Annual allowable cut: 60.1 mill. solid cu.m. incl. bark
Annual total drain, average: 54.6 mill. solid cu.m. incl. bark

Industry

Before World War II Finland was a predominantly agrarian country in the initial stages of industrialization. Moreover, Finnish industry was then still comparatively one-sided. As late as 1938, the forest industry was virtually the only manufacturing industry producing for export, accounting for over 80 % of Finland's total exports.

Diversification of industrial production and increasing exports have been characteristic features of the post-war stages of development. The industrialization process has continued at a particularly rapid pace since 1952, when the war reparations deliveries were completed. In the 1950s and 1960s total production in Finland increased by an average of 5 % a year, and industrial production by about 6 % a year.

Multipurpose machines represent the most highly developed mechanization in forest work. Finnish design and engineering skill deserve credit for producing machines which can be used under difficult conditions.

A result of this development has been that Finland today ranks among the 21 most prosperous countries in the world, measured in terms of per capita income. Another result has been that the share of primary production in total production has declined markedly. The service industries now account for 45 % and manufacturing and construction for over 40 % of total national output.

Distinct evidence of the diversification of industrial production is the growing role of the chemical industry and the rise of the metal and engineering sector to the same level as the forest industry.

The metal sector has become the biggest industrial employer. Practically every third Finn working in industry today is employed by the metal sector. Metal and engineering also lead the value-added statistics, accounting for a good quarter. In terms of gross value of production the forest industry and metal sector stand level.

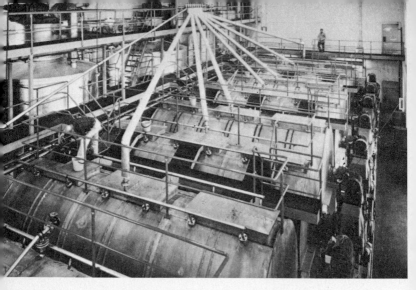

Xylitol is a natural sweetening agent which does not cause dental decay. Finnish scientists developed a method of producing it from birch. A comprehensive 2-year comparative study at university level established that xylitol does not cause caries and that it even stops it in an early stage. The Finnish Sugar Company has the only factory in the world that makes xylitol at present. Xylitol is crystallized in slowly rotating cylinders.

The chemical industry, in particular, has increased its share in the past 20 years. The role of the textile industry, on the other hand, has diminished both as an employer and in total production. The mechanical wood and the pulp and paper branches are geared almost totally to the international market. More than 80 % of the products of the forest industry are exported. The pulp and paper industry accounts for 36 % and the forest industry as a whole for some 44 % of Finland's export earnings. The production capacity of this sector has grown considerably in the past 10 years. Practically every branch has been enlarged and modernised, the pulp and paper branch in particular. Most of the new capacity has been added to existing production units, but there have also been some completely new units.

Another notable structural change has been the move towards higher processing levels. The average Finnish mmll is considerably bigger than its counterpart in other Scandinavian countries. In addition to this important competitive factor, the Finnish forest industry plants have the advantage of extensive integration, and there

Number of Workers, Gross Value of Output and Value Added by Industry in 1979

	Employees		Gross value		Value added	
	Number	%	Mill. Fmk	%	Mill. Fmk	%
Metal	180,900	34	34,215	25	15,260	30
Wood and paper	104,600	20	31,473	23	10,756	21
Textile	64,200	12	7,546	5	3,527	7
Food	59,300	11	22,770	16	5,497	11
Chemical industry	37,400	7	18,724	14	6,000	12
Other	83,300	16	23,940	17	10,639	19
Total	529,700	100	138,668	100	51,679	100

Economically Active Population by Industry in 1975

Industry	Both sexes	Males
Agriculture, hunting, forestry and fishing	318,088	206,049
Mining	8,397	7,305
Manufacturing	543,806	331,852
Electricity, gas and water	179,398	164,588
Trade, restaurants and hotels	310,123	120,140
Transport and communications	160,738	118,991
Financing, insurance, etc.	100,320	37,891
Services	444,342	150,123
Unknown	32,191	23,369
Total	2,121,174	1,179,347

are often several different production lines and stages of processing represented in the same production complex.

Finland is one of the leading European producers of copper and nickel. Other ore resources are zinc, iron, chromium, cobalt and vanadium. Finland produces about 5 % of the world supply of cobalt.

The metal and engineering industry is the leading industrial sector in Finland in terms of value-added production and labour employed. About 60 % of the production is marketed at home and 40 % exported. The metal and engineering sector accounted for 28 % of total exports in 1980. The transport vehicle branch produces ships, lorries and passenger cars, locomotives and railway rolling stock. The major production items in the engineering branch are woodworking industry machines, agricultural and earth-moving machines, and lifts and cranes. The basic-metal-using branch includes the iron and steel industry and processing of non-ferrous metals. Other production branches are electrotechnical and manufacturing. The main marketing areas for several years have been the EFTA and EEC countries, which take two-thirds of the metal industry's total exports today. The leading buyers of Finnish metal and engineering products are Sweden, the Soviet Union, Norway, Britain and the Federal Republic of Germany. The principal export products are vessels, machines, metals and electrical products. The Finnish engineering industry is one of the leading producers of wood-processing machinery in the world. Icebreakers, luxury cruisers, roll on-roll off freighters, car ferries, timber transport ships and oil-drilling rigs are specialities of the shipbuilding industry.

The most important product groups in the chemical industry are the raw chemicals, fuels and lubricants used by industry, fertilizers, plastics, medicines, paints, dyes, technochemical products, soap, man-made fibres and explosives. The plans for developing a petrochemicals industry in Finland began to be implemented at the beginning of 1972. In practice, this means that even in the early stages about half the demand for the more important plastic qualities can be satisfied by products manufactured at home in Finland.

Rauma-Repola Oy is one of the world's leading builders of oil-drilling. It makes three different types of semi-submersible drilling platforms: Pentagone, Aker H-3 and Ocean Ranger. Rigs have been sold to Norway, Britain and the USA. Aker H-3 rigs under construction at Rauma-Repola's Mäntyluoto works.

In the textile and clothing industry the majority of the domestic demand is satisfied by the country's own factories and the same is true to an even greater extent of the leather and rubber industries. Most of the production of food, beverages and tobacco is sold in the home market, but some firms in this sector have won a considerable reputation abroad. The clay, glass and stone industry is also an exporter.

Production and Exports of Forest Industry Products in 1980

Product	Production	Exported
Sawn goods, 1000 cu.m.	10,230	6,939
Plywood, 1000 cu.m.	639	548
Particle board, 1000 cu.m.	809	373
Wallboard, 1000 tons	176	86
Mechanical pulp, 1000 tons	2,346	22
Chemical pulp, 1000 tons	4,606	1,917
Paper, 1000 tons	4,493	3,688
Paperboard, 1000 tons	1,426	1,104

Exports of Metal and Engineering Products in 1980

	mill. Fmk
Ores and concentrates	51
Iron and steel	1,969
Other metals	1,617
Machinery	4,109
Electrical products	2,192
Transport equipment	2,962
Measuring equipment	481
Other	1,647
Total	15,028

Value of Finnish Exports and Imports by Trade Areas in 1980

	Exports mill. Fmk	%	Imports mill. Fmk	%
Total of which	52,793	100.0	58,239	100.0
EFTA	12,423	23.5	10,250	17.6
EEC	20,389	38.6	19,478	33.4
OECD	36,422	69.0	36,144	62.1
CMEA (COMECON)	10,523	19.9	14,399	24.7

Foreign Trade by Main Groups

	Exports, mill. Fmk				
Period	Agri-cultural and other primary products	Wood industry products	Paper industry products	Metal and engineering industry products	Other goods
1975	449	2,177	7,225	5,357	5,039
1976	804	2,892	7,860	6,891	6,058
1977	1,087	3,854	8,798	9,184	8,009
1978	966	4,641	10,402	9,593	9,604
1979	1,366	6,073	12,992	10,342	12,657
1980	1,403	7,742	15,751	11,546	16,353

Domestic Trade

Domestic trade was earlier associated mainly with importing and was chiefly in the hands of foreign business houses or businessmen that had moved to Finland. In 1879, through government action, it became an independent industry and domestic merchants gained the dominant position.

The division of labour has led in trade to a differentiation between wholesale and agency business and retail trading, as in other countries. However, the grouping of Finnish wholesale trade differs considerably from the structure in other Western countries. Trade in consumer goods, in particular, is not elsewhere dominated by such big competing groups as dominate the market in Finland. There are 5 competing groups of this type.

The Finnish State is also engaged in commercial activity, e.g. in agricultural produce. The State-owned Oy Alko Ab has a monopoly in the alcohol trade.

Foreign Trade

Foreign trade has a vital influence on the standard of living in Finland, which has limited natural resources, a one-sided production structure and a rather small domestic market. Finland has to resort to quite heavy importing of goods either not made at home or not worth producing for cost reasons. To pay for its imports, the country exports, mainly forest industry and metal and engineering industry products.

Finland is an associate member of EFTA under the FINEFTA agreement of 1961. This arrangement aimed at safeguarding the competitive standing of the Finnish wood-processing industry in the EFTA area and at

Imports, mill. Fmk				
Raw materials and producer goods	Fuels and lubricants	Manufactures		Other goods
		Investment goods	Consumer goods	
17,058	1,670	5,222	3,989	63
17,828	1,581	4,966	4,103	77
19,124	2,067	4,834	4,600	87
20,431	2,224	4,801	4,830	52
28,878	3,401	5,719	6,133	91
38,622	4,088	7,989	7,440	111

creating the necessary conditions for expanding and diversifying other exports. The Soviet Union was guaranteed most favoured nation status in Finnish foreign trade through a special tariff agreement. In 1973, to protect her competitive ability, Finland signed a free trade agreement with the EEC. The same year she became the first market economy country to sign a cooperation agreement with the CMEA (Comecon). Negotiations were also started with various CMEA member states on the mutual abolition of trade barriers. The first such agreement signed was with Bulgaria, in 1974. These agreements aim at guaranteeing CMEA countries equal standing and opportunities with the EEC in Finnish foreign trade.

Purposeful attempts have been made to diversify the structure of Finnish exports, and these efforts have met with considerable success, especially in the last few years. The proportion of forest industry products in Finland's total exports is still as high as 44 %. But the share of metal and engineering industry products has risen from only a few pre-war per cent to about one-third today. Other manufacturing industries already make up well over 20 % of total exports. The leading branches in this group are textile and clothing and the chemical industry.

In a small industrial country like Finland, imports of machinery, equipment and forms of transport tend to be heavy, due to the concentration of domestic production resources on certain types of product where the country has a good chance of being competitive. In the last few years the largest increase in the value of imports has been in raw materials and production supplies, but almost equally large and greatest in impact was the increase in imports of durable consumer goods (e.g. cars).

Transport and Communications

Investments in communications have, since the middle of the 1950s, accounted for a good fifth of the investments by the State, municipalities and the private sector. The sharp increase in road traffic has taken place at the expense of railway and especially of lake and coastal traffic. The transport and communications sector employs 160,000 persons.

The difficulties in the transport and communications sector are the long distances, lengthy periods when some roads are impassable due to weather conditions, and the periods during which harbours are frozen.

Road traffic
There are 74,600 km of public roads, over 34,000 km of them paved. The number of road vehicles registered is 1.3 million; over 5/6 of them are passenger cars.

Railway traffic is almost entirely a State responsibility. Construction of the railway network began in 1862. The length of the tracks is 9,000 km. The State Railways is the country's major transportation system, employing 29,000 persons. The development of road traffic has faced the railways with competition. The railway system concentrates on the movement of large freight units and flexible long distances, fast passenger traffic between the major population centres and local traffic in the metropolitan region.

Sea traffic
The first actual ports were built in the Middle Ages during the days of the Hanseatic League. But it was not until the 19th century that port services were stimulated by the growing exports of the woodworking industries.

Finland's harbours are largely either export or import harbours, a specialization which has certain inconveniences for land transport. The freezing over of harbours is overcome with icebreakers (since 1890), and many harbours are now kept open throughout the year. Most of Finland's freight and passenger traffic to the outside world goes by sea. The number of ships in the merchant fleet has diminished sharply since World War II, but the average size of the vessels and their capacity have grown. The number of ships in 1979 was 466, the crew totalled around 9,000 and the total tonnage was 2,420,000 GRT.

The need for regular deliveries of goods has resulted in an increase in liner traffic. The overseas lines today run to the east coasts of South and North America. Passenger traffic in the Baltic has grown sharply in recent years.

Air traffic
The domestic air service network of Finland is among

The centre of Finland's domestic and foreign air traffic is Helsinki Airport, which handled 3.2 million passengers in 1979.

the densest in Europe. There are 40 airfields, 24 of which are served by scheduled traffic. There are two main civil aviation companies. Finnair Oy was founded in 1923; the Finnish State is the majority shareowner. It maintains scheduled services to Scandinavia, Central and South Europe, the USSR, and New York, and has regular charter flights to e.g. Kenya, the Mediterranean, Bombay, Canada and the United States. Kar-Air Oy concentrates on charter flights.

Tourism

Finland's potential as a tourist country rests chiefly on its nature sights and the tranquillity it offers as a contrast to many densely populated and highly industrialized countries.

Tourism is becoming quite an important service industry in Finland, bringing in over 5 % of the country's total export earnings. The employment created by the tourist trade is also appreciable. The hotel and restaurant branch employs some 75,000 people and transport and communications about 160,000.

Finland has some 58,000 beds in hotels, motels and hostels. In addition, holiday villages of varying standards have over 14,000 beds; the number of summer cottages for hire is almost 6,000. There are over 300 camping sites.

It is estimated that over 2 million foreign tourists visit Finland yearly. Well over half of them are Scandinavians, mainly Swedes.

Tourism is a part of the State administration. The Finnish Tourist Board is the central authority. It has ten travel information offices of its own abroad and two joint Nordic offices. Tourist spots are described in greater detail on p. 90.

47

SOCIAL WELFARE

Social Policy

Social policy and legislation in Finland generally follow the same lines as in the other Nordic countries and Finland participates in Nordic cooperation also in this sphere. The goal is to guarantee the citizens a reasonable standard of living, social security and contentment. In addition to the traditional labour and social security policy there are many measures relating to health, housing, educational and regional policy. The common aim of all of them is to raise and level the standard of living and to counter the insecurity arising from different risks.

Social progress began in 1906 with the introduction of universal and equal suffrage. The industrial workers had already organized around the turn of the century. The most important milestones in the history of sociopolitical legislation are the 1899 Statute on the Safety of Workers and the Eight Hours Day Act of 1917. Social welfare legislation was broadened greatly in the 1920s and 30s. The Finnish Parliament enacted basic legislation concerning terms of employment in the 20s. Pension legislation got off to a start in 1937 with the National Pensions Act, and the Annual Leave Act was also passed at about the same time. The 60s was another lively period of reform. During this decade the employee pension system was introduced, along with reforms in legislation concerning pensions for civil servants. A general Sickness Insurance Act covering all residents of Finland came into effect in 1964. New legislation concerning pensions for farmers and the self-employed came into force at the beginning of 1970, bringing all the country's 2.3 million employees and self-employed persons within the scope of pension legislation.

Social reforms in the 70s included improvements in the national health system, which provides more or less free care, and the gradual change-over to a free comprehensive school system, as well as a reform of the Labour Protection Act. Social welfare is constantly being developed, with not only the Parliament and the Government, but also employers' and employees' organizations taking an active part in the process.

In the latter part of the 70s, improvements were made in occupational health care and eating facilities at workplaces, among other things, and important new legislation on industrial democracy was enacted. The Annual Leave Act was reformed so that employees having served for five years receive five weeks' annual

leave, of which one week must be taken in winter.
Beginning in 1982 employees will have five weeks'
annual leave after only three years of service. One major
social reform in the early part of the 80s will be a
four-stage improvement in national pension benefits
which is intended to guarantee every pensioner a
minimum income of about 1300–1400 marks a month
by the middle of the decade.

Social Security

Finland's social security provisions fall into three main
categories: social insurance, transfer payments and
personal assistance, with social services evolving into a
fourth category. Social welfare expenditure in 1979
amounted to about 23 per cent of Finland's gross
national product at market prices and was financed as
follows: the State (28 %), municipalities (14 %),
employers (46 %), the insured themselves (7 %) and
service users in fees (5 %). In 1980 social welfare costs
were estimated at about 42,100 million marks. The
primary outlays were for sickness, accidents,
unemployment, old-age, disability, family transfers and
child care. Around 70 % of total expenditure was for old
age, disability, sickness and health care. In the coming
decades Finland will face problems brought on by the
rising percentage of older people in the population. In
1978 there were four pensioners for every ten working
persons; at the turn of the century there will be six
pensioners for every ten working persons, if account is
taken of the expected increase in the number of those
receiving disability pensions. This trend calls for social
policies aimed at ensuring the balanced growth of the
population and favourable treatment for families with
children.

Social Insurance
Social insurance takes the following forms in Finland:
sickness insurance, pension insurance, accident and
occupational disease insurance, unemployment
insurance and motor (third-party) insurance, all of
which are required by law. Compulsory insurance can
be supplemented with voluntary sickness, accident,
retirement, disability, life and other insurance policies.

In 1977 the major labour market organizations
reached an agreement on group life insurance for
employees and public servants which covers all
employees under the age of 65 who are not already
receiving old-age pensions. If an employee dies while
still in service or within three years of termination of
employment, his survivors receive compensation. In
1981, for example, a basic lump sum of 31,360 marks

was to be paid to the spouse of any employee (male or female) dying before the age of 40, with a supplement of 8,300 marks for each minor child.

The Sickness Insurance Act, which came into effect in 1964, covers all residents of Finland and provides for treatment of illness at little or no charge. Sick persons between 16 and 64 years of age are paid a per diem allowance after eight days of illness and up to a maximum of 300 workdays. Mothers receive maternity benefit for up to 258 workdays. With certain provisions, fathers may also receive paternity benefit for up to 48 days, in which case the mother's benefit is reduced by a corresponding amount. The Sickness Insurance Act has been amended so that per diem allowances and maternity benefits are taxable income as of 1982, when substantial increases in both also come into effect. The per diem allowance for sick persons will be 80 % of normal income, as will the maternity benefit (after a certain period of transition). The minimum per diem allowance is 27.50 marks.

At the same time the Sickness Insurance Act was amended, legislation concerning accident and motor insurance was similarly changed so that as of 1982 compensation received under the relevant acts is taxable income. Benefit increases were also provided.

The oldest form of statutory social insurance in Finland is employee accident insurance, which has been required by law since 1895. has subsequently been amended to extend the range of workers covered and benefits provided, and the term employee accident has been widened to include occupational diseases. The Supervision of Labour Protection Act, passed in 1973, has had a major effect on health conditions at places of work. The latest step in expanding accident insurance is legislation providing coverage for farmers, which will come into effect in July 1982.

Accident insurance legislation was further amended to provide full compensation for loss of earnings resulting from an accident. Motor insurance has traditionally provided such compensation.

The Finnish health care system ensures that hospitalization costs are evenly distributed among the population, as most of the country's hospital beds are in institutions operated by the State or joint authorities. Fees for services cover only a very small percentage of actual health care costs. The 1972 Public Health Act regulates health care and costs. The Act also provides for free dental care for children under 17.

Finland has a dual pension system. The national pension guarantees a decent livelihood, while an additional employee pension based on previous earnings helps maintain the pensioner's standard of living. Persons who have been employed receive both types of

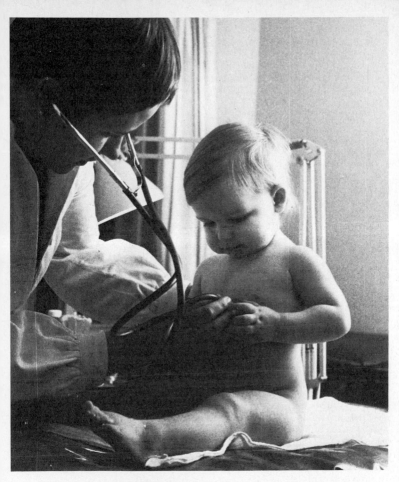

Municipal maternity and child welfare centres have taken care of the health care of expectant mothers and children aged 0–6 years for over 50 years. Medical examinations, pre-natal training, general health supervision and vaccinations are free. The welfare centres are numerous enough to make them accessible to everyone.

pension; those who have never held jobs covered by pension schemes receive only the national pension, which varies according to the other income and property of the pensioner and his spouse. For a single person living alone and with no other income, the full national pension in Helsinki on 1 July 1981 came to 1,288 marks a month tax free. Recipients of national pensions are also elligible for housing assistance.

The National Pension Act, which was passed in 1937 and amended in 1956, covers all residents of Finland over 16 years of age, regardless of nationality. The national pension is a social pension based largely on need and income. A four-stage reform of pension benefits was started in 1980 and is intended to make the national pension independent of need and income criteria by the middle of the 80s. The goal is to guarantee every pensioner an individual national pension affected only by the pensioner's own employee pension. Finland initiated its system of earnings-related pensions in the early 1960s, though seamen and State and municipal employees already had pension schemes by then. In 1962 pension legislation covering people working in the private sector came into effect. Pensions under this legislation are tied to the employee's earnings and length of employment. Pension schemes for government, municipal and church employees were also brought into conformance with the basic Employee Pension Act around this time. In the early 70s, farmers and self-employed persons were included in the employee pension scheme.

The full employee pension is presently 60−66 % of earnings before retirement. In order to receive the full pension, an employee must work 30 years in the case of public servants and 40 years for those in the private sector.

Persons entitled to pensions are paid according to the National Pension Act and the Employee Pension Acts. Old age pensions usually begin at 65 years of age, disability pensions are provided for those incapacitated for work, and unemployment pensions are paid to people who have been out of work for long periods of time. Old age pensions begin at an earlier age in some cases; public servants, for example, can retire at 63. A person may receive a full disability pension, which is as much as his old age pension would be, if his ability to work or earn his living has decreased by at least 60 %. Persons whose earning ability has decreased by 40−59 % may receive partial pensions while continuing to work. Unemployment pensions are intended to help unemployed persons aged 55−64. Other legislation provides for the payment of a special pension to war veterans over the age of 55 in cases of disability because of weak health and if the recipient has a low income.

Survivor's pension provisions cover widows (and widowers in the case of public servants) and children. The Employee Pension Acts ensure pensions for children up to 18, while the General Survivor's Pension Act covers children up to 16 years of age. Children receive a survivor's pension following the death of either or both parents.

Unemployment insurance covers all persons over 16

who belong to the labour force. The State pays unemployment benefits to any person who reports to his local employment office and has been out of work through no fault of his own for at least five consecutive working days. The unemployment allowance varies from 36 to 52 marks a day, according to the number of dependants. Benefits are paid until the recipient finds work. An employee belonging to a national trade union may receive unemployment assistance from his union for a maximum of 200 days a year. Unemployment assistance may be paid for a maximum of 500 days and amounts to 42—59 marks a day, according to the number of dependants. Both types of benefit are tax free. Older employees who have become unemployed through no fault of their own may receive severance pay, with the amount depending of the employee's age and length of employment.

Finland is one of the leading countries in pediatrics. Heart examinations of infants at the Meilahti Hospital, University Central Hospital, Helsinki.

National pensions, general survivor's pensions, veteran's pensions, unemployment compensation, pension-related housing assistance and sickness insurance costs are all covered by tax revenues or social security contributions, which closely resemble taxes. An employee pension is simply part of the employee's salary which is set aside for use at a later time. Employee pension premiums are paid by the employer, who is also responsible for occupational accident and group life insurance premiums for his employees. Contributions to the unemployment insurance scheme are paid jointly by the employer, government and the insured himself. Motor insurance premiums are the responsibility of individual vehicle owners.

The most notable feature of Finland's present social insurance system is that pensions and other benefits vary on the basis of previous income, and this will be even more true in the future. Employee pensions, sickness insurance benefits and compensation from accident or motor insurance are all earnings-related, for example. The aim is of course to maintain the recipient's previous standard of living. On the other hand, the national pension, war veteran's pension and unemployment benefit are intended to guarantee a basic livelihood, regardless of previous earnings, for those with little other income.

Transfer payments
Transfer payments are made in order to level living costs by means of fixed benefits paid out of public funds to certain groups of people, without regard to individual means. Transfer payment recipients fall into two main groups, families and young persons, though benefits are also paid to certain invalids and the families of persons doing compulsory military service.

The primary aim of family transfer payments is to make it easier for people to set up families and to help families with young children get along. Maternity benefits, child benefits, special child allowances, assistance for parents staying at home to care for their children, child support payments and municipal housing assistance for families with children all serve this end. The Child Benefit Act, which came into effect in 1948, provides for the payment from State funds of a set amount for each child under the age of 16, regardless of the family's means. In 1981 yearly benefits were as follows: 1,432 marks for the first child, 1,656 for the second, 1,928 for the third and 2,460 for the fourth and each subsequent child. A supplementary benefit of 824 marks a year is paid for each child under 3.

Families also receive other benefits in the form of tax relief and assistance when the couple get married, when they have children and when the children are in school.

The maternity grant is one of the oldest forms of transfers, dating back to 1937, and is given to all mothers, regardless of means, either as a lump sum or in the form of clothing and other supplies for the baby.

This category of benefits also includes payments to the families of men doing their military service to make up for loss of income and special benefits for the blind and other people with serious handicaps who are working as best they can to support themselves and their families. In 1981 the yearly allowance was 10,476 for the blind, 7,284 for persons with 2/3 disabilities and 5,292 for other handicapped persons.

Study grants and State-supported loans are provided to help young people continue their education after the comprehensive school.

Housing assistance is intended to ensure families with small incomes a reasonable level of housing at affordable prices. Besides granting housing allowances, the State also funds long-term, low-rate housing loans, regulates and supervises rents and has new apartments built.

Personal assistance

The aim of personal assistance is to aid individuals in social difficulties, regardless of their employment status. Personal assistance in Finland has increasingly come under governmental supervision. Personal assistance differs from social insurance and transfer payments in that the emphasis is on individual cases. The State and the municipalities are officially responsible for this work, while the church has a semi-official responsibility and various civic organizations lend assistance in a voluntary capacity. The local body in charge of this type of assistance is the municipal welfare board, which distributes funds through the local welfare office.

Present-day personal assistance can be divided into two types of activity: direct assistance aimed at ensuring a sufficient level of income, and assistance for children, young people and persons with adjustment problems. The Child Protection Act and other legislation provide means of looking after the health, legal rights and economic condition of children and young people.

Personal assistance can also be classified according to whether or not the recipient is institutionalized. In the 80s developments are leading to greater and greater emphasis on assistance outside institutions. Most assistance for adults is already of this nature, since the relevant legislation stipulates that whenever possible, the recipient should be allowed to live at home or with relatives. Alcoholics, for example, may also receive institutionalized assistance, however.

Social services may be thought of as that group of welfare activities which do not involve actual monetary assistance. Social services are evolving into a category of their own and continue to play an increasingly important role in today's modern service society. Examples are Finland's network of maternity and post-natal clinics, child guidance clinics, marriage and family counselling clinics, services for unwed mothers and their children, child day-care centres, home help services, vocational counselling for young persons and legal assistance for the needy.

Services for the aged and disabled are constantly growing in importance: in 1980 Finland had nearly 600,000 old-age pensioners and about 250,000 people on disability pensions. Besides the fact that more people are now receiving pensions, the average life expectancy has also risen, which creates still new challenges for social services.

National Health Service

The central office of the health service is the National Board of Health, which is responsible for the medical staff and services. The administrative network subordinated to the central office comprises the social and health departments of the administrative districts (provinces).

Health services are primarily organized by local authorities (municipalities) and subsidized by the State. One or more municipalities form a health centre district, which organizes the primary services for the area. These services include maternity and child health care, school and student health services, occupational health, dental health, and ambulance services.

Central and local hospitals are responsible for hospital care. In Finland there are 689 hospitals, four of which are university central hospitals.

In recent years the development of primary health care has been particularly emphasized. Important divisions are family planning, health education and occupational health. Mental health services form an integral part of primary care and they are provided by health centres and mental health bureaux. Health centres and hospitals provide about 75 per cent of primary medical care in Finland. The rest is supplied through private practice.

The number of personnel working in health care is over 100,000. There are 8,500 physicians (18 physicians per 10,000 of inhabitants), 3,500 dentists (8 dentists per 10,000 of inhabitants) and 27,000 public health and other nurses.

Except in the case of dental treatment for adults,

health centre visits are free, including all necessary
laboratory examinations and X-rays. A visit to a hospital
outpatient clinic costs 19 Fmk and a hospital bed 21–90
Fmk a day. Health care expenditure accounted for 7 per
cent of the GNP in 1977.

There are 563 pharmacies in Finland where medicine
is dispensed. People pay a part of the cost of medicine
themselves; sickness insurance pays the rest. Medicine is
provided free of charge to some long-term patients. The
average life expectancy in Finland is on the same level
as that in other industrialized countries of Europe. The
mortality rate for middle-aged men in Finland remains
higher than in the other Nordic countries.
Cardiovascular diseases are the main cause of death;
tumours rank second and accidents and violence third.
Infant mortality is very low in Finland. In 1979 it was
8.7 per 1,000 live births.

Employment and Work Safety

The Finnish economy has undergone an extensive
restructuring process since World War II, away from
primary and towards secondary industry. In 1979, only
every eighth Finn gained his livelihood from agriculture
and forestry. One in every three Finns was employed in
the manufacturing sector. Commerce, transport and
communications and the service trades employed a
higher proportion of the labour force than industry and
building in the 1960s when emigration to Sweden was at
its highest because of regional unemployment. There is
still unemployment in the development areas. To
remedy this situation, the State offers tax reliefs and
provides interest subsidies and guarantees for loans
taken for new investment projects and the expansion of
existing productive undertakings in the two
development   zones" of the country. The Regional
Development Fund Ltd. (f. 1971) grants credits to the
development areas. Vocational training, re-training and
guidance have been intensified in these areas. On the
other hand, migration of labour to jobs in the south is
supported with social grants.

The collective bargaining system really became
established in Finland during World War II. The
agreements were generally concluded by branches and
covered almost all workers. In the 1960s, the
agreements were made at the national level with the
Government as a participant. These agreements covered
wage increases, price controls, charges of a tax-like
nature, and rent controls. The 1971 agreement
guaranteed all employees of 18 years of age and over a
minimum wage and an annual holiday of 4 weeks. The
earnings level has risen steadily under subsequent

agreements, but inflation has swallowed a considerable part of the nominal increase. Since 1973, employees have been paid a return-from-holiday bonus which was initially 20 % and is now 40–60 % of the pay entitlement for the holiday period. Landmarks in the 1970s have been the new Employment Act, which considerably improves the security of the unemployed, the establishment of the National Board of Trade and Consumer Interests, which supervises prices, and the National Board of Labour Protection. The objectives ahead are the implementation of industrial democracy (worker participation).

An amendment to the Law on Working Hours established the 40-hour working week in 1970.

Disputes over collective agreements are handled by the Labour Court (f. 1946), whose verdict is final. The State Arbitrator for Industrial Conflicts and district arbitrators, all appointed by the President of the Republic, mediate in the event of strikes, threatened strikes, lock-outs, etc.

Considerable attention has been paid of late to work safety. The object is to eliminate accident and health risks and to increase job satisfaction at the work site. The National Board of Labour Protection was established in 1973 for all these matters. The lowest instance of the system is the work safety committee (at work sites with at least 20 employees) and the work safety delegate (for 10 employees).

The social welfare system in Finland undergoes continuous development, in which not only the Government and the Parliament participate, but also the employers and employees through the settlements reached by their respective organizations.

At the end of the 1970s, improvements were made in the system of occupational health care and in the on-the-job lunch programme, and a law was passed on cooperation between employers and employees in industrial democracy.

Housing Policy

Almost all Finnish towns and especially the southern urban centres suffer from a housing shortage, partly because of the structural changes that have occurred in society. This is in spite of the fact that entire new developments have been added to the major towns since World War II. In 1949, the State began to promote housing production under the ARAVA (State Housing Production Committee) scheme, which provided low-interest, long-term loans to municipalities, corporations and private individuals. The ARAVA laws were superseded in 1966 by a new Housing Production

Act. ARAVA activity is now continued by the National Housing Board, which is responsible for the distribution of State loans and the overall programming, supervision and managements of housing production, and follows non-subsidised housing production.

The planning of housing policy has gained special emphasis in the 1970s as it has been linked with greater entities, that is to say urban, community and regional planning. Urbanization has influenced the trend of housing policy and the weight now rests on the problems of towns and population centres. The dominant feature of urban building has been high-rise buildings and, within them, small dwelling units. The authorities are now trying to correct this situation. Finland has one of the highest housing densities in Europe.

The housing completion rate in the 1960s was an average of 37,000 units a year. This rose in the 1970s to 60,000 units. In spite of this, there is still a housing shortage and housing costs are high.

SCHOOLS AND EDUCATION

The Finnish school system has developed a great deal since the late 1960s, in terms of both structure and curriculum. Reforms have been carried out at all levels, though some changes will only be completed in the latter half of the 80s.

Finland's educational system can be divided into four levels: pre-school education, compulsory education (the nine-year comprehensive school), upper secondary education and higher education, which includes universities and other such institutions. Adult education is intended to complement the work done at the last three levels.

The administration of educational and cultural affairs is generally the responsibility of the Ministry of Education and authorities under its jurisdiction. In recent years, education, science and culture have accounted for 17−19 % of Finland's total State budget.

The title page of an ABC book from 1828.

Pre-school education

Finland does not provide schools for children under the age of seven, but a growing proportion of children take part in organized day care, which comes under the jurisdiction of the Ministry of Social Welfare and Health. The goal of children's day care, according to law, is to promote development and opportunities for learning, to aid the home in carrying out its educational tasks and to balance out differences in learning ability due to family background.

In 1980 about 120,000 children attended day-care centres maintained by local government authorities. This was over one-fourth of the country's children aged 0−6. Especially in developing population centres, however, demand outstrips supply considerably.

An ABC book in the Lapp language from 1967. ABC books in the language of the northern Lapps and Skolt Lapps have also been published.

The comprehensive school

Finland has a compulsory nine-year comprehensive school, which is divided into a six-year lower stage and a three-year upper stage. Every child in Finland must attend the comprehensive school or complete a similar curriculum.

Children go into the first class of the comprehensive school in August of the year in which they reach the age of seven. Schooling is completely free of charge, with pupils receiving books and school supplies, as well as free school meals. Pupils who have more than five kilometres to go are provided transportation to and from school, and in the lower grades transportation is sometimes provided in other cases as well. Nearly one-third of Finland's comprehensive school pupils benefit from such services.

The municipalities are responsible for arranging education at this level. State assistance is provided for this purpose and presently covers around 70 % of comprehensive school costs.

Teachers in the lower stage of the comprehensive school receive a broad pedagogical training and are thus able to teach all the subjects offered in the first six years, with some exceptions. Depending on the size and staff of the school, some teachers may specialize, however. Teachers in the last three years of the comprehensive school are generally responsible for one or two subjects in which they have specialized. Since the 1970s, teacher training has been the duty of universities and similar institutions.

Pupils in the lower stage receive 21–26 hours of instruction per five-day week, while pupils in the upper stage receive 30 hours. All pupils are given the same instruction in the lower stage, but in the upper stage pupils may be divided into two or three sets in mathematics and foreign languages. The child's guardians decide which syllabus they would like their

The new schooling system aims at bringing the pupils into closer contact with social activities at an early stage. During the country-wide Press Week in 1976 children studied the contents of newspapers, their make-up, how to conduct interviews, etc.

child to take in each case and also select optional courses (up to four hours a week) for their child.

Compulsory subjects in the lower stage include religion, environmental studies, Finnish or Swedish, a foreign language (usually English), history and social studies, civics, maths, natural history and geography, PE, music, art and handicrafts. The same subjects, with the exception of environmental studies, are also compulsory in the upper stage, where pupils must also take a second foreign language (usually Swedish, or Finnish in the case of Swedish-speaking Finns), physics, chemistry and home economics.

In 1980 Finland had about 620,000 pupils in its comprehensive school system.

Pupils who have completed the comprehensive school are presently qualified to continue their studies in any part of the upper secondary level, with certain exceptions. The comprehensive school is now being developed so that by 1986 there will be no limitations regarding qualifications for further study at this level.

Henrik Gabriel Porthan (1739–1804), historian. Was the first to study Finnish history scientifically.

Upper secondary education

The academically oriented upper secondary school lasts three years and leads up to a matriculation examination, which is the usual prerequisite for admittance to any institution of higher learning. Almost all of Finland's upper secondary schools are maintained by municipalities. At present just under half of the country's 16-year-olds go on to the upper secondary school. However, about one in every five pupils subsequently drops out. In 1980 Finland had about 110,000 pupils in upper secondary schools, over seven times as many as in 1950 and about twice as many as in 1965. Six out of ten pupils are girls.

In recent years the number of pupils completing the matriculation examination has levelled off at about 25,000 a year. The exam is arranged nationwide, but passing marks do not entitle the pupil automatically to a place at a university. At present about 40 % of those who have completed the matriculation exam are admitted to institutions of higher learning. The others may continue their studies in vocational schools. In 1979, for example, about one-fourth of the pupils entering vocational schools had completed the matriculation exam.

There will be a switch-over to modular teaching in the upper secondary school in 1982–84. All pupils will take Finnish, Swedish, one or two other languages, physics, chemistry, geography, biology, history and social studies, religion, art or music, PE and health. A number of optional courses will also be offered, especially in the last form. Pupils will have an average of 30 courses (at

62

38 hours each) in the first two forms and about 20 courses in the final form. The various parts of the matriculation examination will be given during the spring of the third year, as at present.

Vocational schools are the other main part of secondary level education. This category includes schools and institutes in the areas of agriculture and forestry, technology, transportation and communications, commerce and secretarial work, and various services. About 129,000 pupils attended vocational schools in 1979, with over one-half studying in technical fields. Vocational schools are maintained by the State, local government and private firms and societies.

A reform of vocational education will be taking place in 1982—88. Studies will be based on the comprehensive school syllabus. All pupils will study the same subjects for the first year, during which instruction in liberal arts subjects will amount to at least 500 hours or almost half of the corresponding figure for the first form of the upper secondary school. Compulsory subjects will include Finnish, Swedish, one other language, maths, physics, chemistry, civics, PE, health, and art and environmental studies.

After one year of basic studies, pupils will specialize in some area of work for one to four years of further studies. Certain groups of pupils will then be eligible for admittance to institutions of higher learning in their particular fields.

Pupils at the upper secondary level must meet the costs of studying themselves. The State provides assistance in many ways, however. In recent years low-interest study loans have been given to nearly half those attending vocational schools and not quite 5 % of those attending the upper secondary school, who are usually able to live at home because of the density of the school network.

Higher education

Finland's first university, the former Turku Academy, was established in 1640. After the Turku fire (1827), in which the Academy suffered serious damage, and for political reasons, the Academy was moved to Helsinki, the new capital of the Grand Duchy of Finland. Here it began operating in 1828 under the name of Finland's Imperial Alexander University.

Before Finland gained independence, two other institutions of higher learning were opened: the Helsinki University of Technology (1908) and the Helsinki School of Economics (1911). The country presently has 18 university-level institutions and three art schools. In

1980 about 83,000 students were enrolled. The largest institutions were the University of Helsinki (22,000), the University of Turku (8,800), the University of Tampere (8,500), the Helsinki University of Technology (7,400), the University of Oulu (7,100) and the University of Jyväskylä (5,900).

Each year about 12,000 new students enter university-level education, with 11,000 taking studies which lead to lower university degrees. Since the demand for places at universities exceeds the number available, applicants must take entrance examinations in the subject of their choice. Admission criteria also include marks received in the matriculation examination and from the upper secondary school. A set number of university places is set aside for students who have not completed the matriculation examination.

University tuition is free of charge in Finland, but students must meet normal living costs and pay for their own books, unless they choose to borrow them from university or other libraries or study them at university reading rooms. The State provides study grants to some students and also backs low-interest student loans. In addition the State supports people in higher education indirectly by subsidizing student meals, student housing projects and student health centres, for example.

Higher education is also provided by summer universities operating in June through August, which offer courses for university degrees and further professional studies of an in-service nature. Summer universities are generally open to all and do not select their students on the basis of previous education. They are financed by funds from local and State government. In recent years Finland's summer universities have attracted around 40,000 students annually, with about one-third of this number being regular university students.

Adult education

Most people take part in adult education in order to improve their basic general education, to receive basic or advanced vocational training or to develop themselves in view of working or leisure-time needs.

The largest group of adult education institutions includes workers' and civic institutes (both names referring to the same type of thing), which are usually maintained by local government. In 1979 Finland had 270 such institutions, with about 520,000 students. Classes are usually held in the evenings. Studies do not provide formal qualifications, but students may be able to pass exams at the upper secondary or lower university level on the basis of such studies. Courses of a vocational nature are becoming more common.

Folk high schools and academies are boarding schools which provide liberal arts, social and vocational education and practical training. In 1978 about 6,200 young people were in schools of this type, and over 25,000 persons attended short-term courses offered by them.

National cultural organizations, most of which operate in conjunction with political parties, maintain study group activities at special study institutes, for which State support is available with certain stipulations. In 1978 nearly 370,000 persons attended seminars, lectures and study groups at such institutes, with about one-half involved in study group activities.

Adult education services are also provided by evening schools, where persons 16 years of age and older can upgrade their education and complete the upper secondary school syllabus. Public libraries, which are maintained by the municipalities with State support, arrange lectures, exhibitions, concerts and other cultural events. Adult education programmes on radio and television have been greatly expanded in the past decade. Courses are usually accompanied by written materials.

The most important form of occupational training for adults is vocational courses, which are the responsibility of the employment and vocational education authorities. Courses vary in length from two weeks to eighteen months and are intended to improve the vocational ability of people who are out of work or in danger of losing their jobs and thus to ensure them a place in the labour market. Since the latter half of the 70s, employment training has also been arranged for jobless persons with university degrees. Such courses are free of charge, and participants even receive a per diem allowance.

Although over 60 % of Finland's working age population lacks vocational training, only one-fourth of those participating in adult education have taken part in occupational training schemes. One central goal in developing the adult education system is in fact to increase the amount of vocational training provided.

Research

Scientific research work is carried out at State research institutes, private research centres and institutions of higher learning. In 1977 business enterprises (including those in which the State or local government owned major shares) financed about 52 % of the nation's research (661 million marks), while the public sector backed 47 % (608 million marks). Total research expenditures presently amount to just over 1 % of the gross national product. About 90 % of the research outlays in the private sector in 1977 went for studies concerning industry and mining. Over 40 % of research expenditures in the public sector in the same year resulted from projects carried out at institutions of higher learning.

Scientific research comes under the jurisdiction of the Ministry of Education, which is generally responsible for science policy and the development of basic research. The main body concerned with the administration of research is the Academy of Finland, which includes a central board and six national research councils. The Academy plans scientific research work and appoints scientists to research positions and professorships for set periods of time. It also distributes grants particularly for pure scientific research.

The State Board of Sciences is responsible for dealing with important questions related to the promotion of scientific research and education. The Board is chaired by the Prime Minister and includes six other Cabinet members and seven experts in the field of scientific research.

The library of the University of Helsinki is one of the stylistically purest of C.L. Engel's Empire style buildings in the centre of the capital.

International Exchange of Trainees

International exchange of trainees helps to increase contact, interaction and exchange of know-how between countries. The responsibility for the exchange of trainees lies with the Ministry of Labour. The exchanges are generally based on the principle of reciprocity.

Official agreements on the exchange of trainees have been made with the Netherlands, Belgium, Brazil, Italy, Austria, France and Switzerland. Trainees are exchanged within the framework of unofficial cooperation agreements with e.g. Britain, the Federal Republic of Germany, the United States and Canada. Training of students of technology is organized through the International Association for the Exchange of Students for Technical Experience (IAESTE), of which Finland is a member.

CULTURE

Folk Culture

The Finnish rural population has always been a vital element of the nation. The farmers were never serfs and large manorial estates were few. Thus the greater part of the cultivated land has always been owned by independent farmers, and this ancient heritage of freedom has left its mark on the folk culture — an important part of Finnish culture as a whole. Farmhouses were roomy and not without architectural merit. The rooms were decorated with fine textiles, especially the traditional woven ryijy». The furniture was often home-made, for the Finnish farmer has always been skilful with wood.

Farming communities formed themselves into villages, which held title to extensive areas, including hunting grounds, fishing rights, etc. It was here that the native oral tradition of epic poetry, legends, stories, proverbs and riddles began and was preserved until it attracted the attention of scholars at the beginning of the 19th century. The man chiefly responsible for compiling this Finnish folk literature was Elias Lönnrot. The Kalevala, published by him in 1835, did much to raise the Finnish language to its rightful position and to stimulate national consciousness. Since Lönnrot's days so much literature of this type has been collected that the folklore archives of the Society of Finnish Literature in Helsinki have developed into the largest of their kind in the world (1,550,000 catalogued items). Between 1908

Elias Lönnrot (1802—1884), physician, folklorist, philologist. Collected folk poetry from which he compiled the national epic Kalevala (1835 and 1849) and Kanteletar (1840).

The English translation of the Kalevala from 1907.

In the Middle Ages about 80 greystone churches were built in Finland. The picture shows the 15th century church of St. Anne in Kumlinge, in the eastern Åland islands.

and 1950, 33 volumes were issued under the title The Ancient Poetry of the Finnish People», the largest work of its kind ever published in any language.

There is a wealth of Finnish folk songs, which were originally sung to the accompaniment of native instruments such as the kantele (resembling a zither).

Finland's folk culture is displayed in all its variety at the National Museum in Helsinki and in some 400 provincial museums. The largest open – air museums are at Seurasaari, an island in Helsinki, where entire farm buildings have been re-erected in their original form, and Convent Hill in Turku, where a section of the town dating from the 18th century has been preserved.

Science

Since the latter half of the 19th century one of the main objectives of scientific research in Finland has been to create a clear and detailed picture of Finland as a country and a nation. This research has also resulted in findings of international importance. Finnish geologists have done much to create a coherent picture of Fenno-Scandia. A.K. Cajander's (1879–1943) theory of forest types has been applied to forests in countries with very different conditions from those prevailing in Finland. The first survey of Finland's forest resources – incidentally the first of its kind in the world – was conducted by Yrjö Ilvessalo (1892–) in 1921–24. Subsequently it has served as a pattern for other countries.

Carrying on the work of M.A. Castrén, the Finno-Ugrian Society has enriched the study of the Ural-Altaic languages.

Finnish researchers have made a valuable contribution to the study of folk poetry and folk tales. The typing system for folk tales devised by A. Aarne (1867–1925), which is used all over the world today, was of decisive importance.

Edward Westermarck (1862–1939), who studied the origin and history of marriage and the origin and development of moral ideals, had an international reputation among sociologists. Finland has also produced a number of prominent orientalists – e.g. Knut Tallqvist (1865–1949) and Armas Salonen (1915–). Väinö Auer (1895–1981) has led several Finnish and Argentinian geographical expeditions. S.R. Karsten (1879–1956), the sociologist, studied the life and early history of South American Indians. Important contributions to astronomy have been made by Yrjö Väisälä (1895–1971), inventor of the interferometer, an instrument for measuring base-lines to an accuracy of some hundredths of a millimetre, and K.F. Sundman (1873–1949), who was the first scientist to solve the three-body" problem. The best known of the Finnish school of mathematics are Lars Ahlfors (1907–), P.J. Myrberg (1892–1976) and Rolf Nevanlinna (1895–1980). Thanks to their work, Finland is one of the leading countries in the study of the theory of functions. A.I. Virtanen (1895–1973) was awarded the Nobel Prize for chemistry in 1945.

One of the leading names in Finnish medical science is Arvo Ylppö (1887–), who has done pioneering work in pediatrics and the study of premature infants. The neurophysiologist Ragnar Granit (1900–), who has been working in Sweden since 1940, was awarded the Nobel Prize in 1967 for his work on colour vision. Georg Henrik von Wright (1916–) and Jaakko Hintikka

Matthias Alexander Castrén (1813–52) founded the branch of Finno-Ugrian philology. He carried out scientific research into as many as 40 languages and dialects of the Finno-Ugrian, Turco-Mongolian and Tungus groups.

Nils Adolf Erik Nordenskiöld (1832–1901), geographer, Arctic explorer. Made several voyages of exploration to Spitzbergen, Greenland, Iceland and North Siberia. Discovered the long-sought North-East Passage in 1878.

Artturi Iivari Virtanen, biochemist. Studied albumin production and biologic nitrogen engagement; invented the system of preserving fresh fodder (AIV fodder) and methods of improving the quality of butter and cheese.

(1929–) have gained international renown in the fields of philosophy and logic.

Literature

The oldest Finnish literature is epic poetry, legends, tales and proverbs which have been passed on by word of mouth. This was followed in the Middle Ages by minor, mainly religious literature in Latin. The Reformation activated the development of written Finnish and literature in the vernacular. The foundation was laid by Mikael Agricola's (1510–1557) ABC (1543) and the Finnish translation of the New Testament (1548). Until the early 19th century Finnish-language literature was mainly of a spiritual and popular educational nature; the most significant fiction was in the Swedish language. It was not until the Helsinki romanticism trend (1830–1860) that a conscious effort was made to create a national culture and Finnish-language literature. At the head of the movement were J.V. Snellman (1806–1881), statesman and political philosopher, and Elias Lönnrot (1802–1884), who collected the treasures of Finland's old poetry into the Kalevala and Kanteletar. J.L. Runeberg (1804–1877) and Zacharias Topelius (1818–1898) produced new national literature in the Swedish language. The period of Late Romanticism (1860–1880) gave Finnish literature its most significant author, Aleksis Kivi (1834–1872). His epic masterpiece "Seven brothers" (1870; translated into over 20 languages) and his plays contain Finnish artistic prose and dramatic literature which are still unsurpassed. Realism arrived in Finland in the 1880s: Minna Canth (1844–1897) exposed the injustices suffered by the proletariat and women; Juhani Aho (1861–1921) was a portrayer of nature and the life of the people, and a master of style; Teuvo Pakkala (1862–1925) described the poor and the children of small towns with psychological discernment.

The turn of the century was dominated by Karelianism which derived its inspiration from virgin wildernesses and the Karelian lands with their Kalevala songs. This era gave Finnish poetry its greatest talent, Eino Leino (1878–1926), whose "Whitsongs» (1903, 1916) was a brilliant synthesis of the spirit of the age. The great portrayers of the people, Johannes Linnankoski (1869–1913), Joel Lehtonen (1881–1934) and F.E. Sillanpää (1888–1964), dominated the prose literature of the first decades of the present century. Sillanpää's works are characterized by a biological and natural mystical view of man. He was awarded the Nobel Prize in 1939. His main works are "Meek Heritage" (1919) and "The Maid Silja" (1931). Maria Jotuni

Aleksis Kivi, the greatest Finnish author.

(1880—1943) is one of the greatest names of Finnish short stories and her miniature plays give her the same status in our dramatic art. For Swedish-language literature the beginning of the century was a Renaissance, especially in lyric poetry. The outstanding name is Edith Södergran (1882—1923), the forerunner of Finnish modernism. Other modernists of that period were the social aesthete Elmer Diktonius (1896—1961) and the expressionistic dadaist Gunnar Björling (1887—1960). The writer who won the greatest international fame in his time is Mika Waltari (1908—79). His great historical novels (e.g. "The Egyptian "1945) have been translated into 25 languages. Influential names between the two world wars were Pentti Haanpää (1906—1955), who revealed a primitive strength as an interpreter of rural man, nature and animals, and Toivo Pekkanen (1902—1957), the objective portrayer of industrializing society.

Johan Ludvig Runeberg (1804—77), poet. Became famous as a Finnish national poet — largely through his Tales of Ensign Ståhl. The opening poem of the series is Our Land, now the Finnish National Anthem.

The wars, territorial cessions and the completely changed internal and foreign policy situation compelled a national self-searching and re-evaluation of history among the writers. Leading this mainstream was Väinö Linna (1920—). His novel "The Unknown Soldier" (1954) was an entirely new, honest view of the war and the ordinary soldier. His crofter trilogy "Täällä Pohjantähden alla" (Here under the North Star, 1959—1962) is a socio-historical cross-section of the vicissitudes of the Finnish people. Veijo Meri (1928—) has gained an international reputation. He began as a depicter of war and is one of the most singular narrators of his generation; his works are characterised by grotesque, often cruel humour. The 1950s was a decade of modernism, with lyric poetry as the pioneer. The leading characters were and still are Tuomas Anhava (1927—), Eeva-Liisa Manner (1921—) and, above all, Paavo Haavikko (1931—), lyricist, prose writer, playwright. Pentti Saarikoski (1937—) and Anselm Hollo (1934—) may be mentioned among younger writers. The latter, having lived a long time in England and the United States, also writes poetry in English and is a well-known translator of Finnish lyrics. There has been a strengthening social trend in prose literature since the 1960s. Its leading spokesmen are Hannu Salama (1936—), Alpo Ruuth (1943—) and Lassi Sinkkonen (1937—1976).

In the forefront of the Finnish-Swedish authors today are Tito Colliander (1904—), Christer Kihlman (1930—), Marianne Alopaeus (1918—) and Henrik Tikkanen (1924—). Tove Jansson (1914—) is known world-wide for her lovable and wise Moomin troll books.

Frans Emil Sillanpää, author. Wrote novels and short stories. Nobel Prize 1939.

Music

Jean Sibelius, composer. Works: Kullervo Symphony, En Saga, the four Lemminkäinen legends, Carelia Suite, Finlandia, 7 symphonies, violin concerto, the string quartet Voces Intimae, stage music Pelléas and Melisande, Belsazar's Feast, The Tempest. About 100 songs for solo voice and 40 for choir.

Folk music is associated largely with rural society. The systematic collection of tunes began in the first half of the 19th century. Over 100,000 of them have been assembled. The kantele (Finnish musical instrument, originally with five strings over a horizontal sounding board, and plucked by hand) is the national musical instrument. The great international folk music festival of Kaustinen is staged every summer.

The oldest memorials of the history of music are Catholic church music from the turn of the 12th century. *Piae cantiones,* published in 1582, are medieval school and church songs in Latin. The first publications of Protestant choral singing date from the 16th century.

The first well-known composers were Erik Tulindberg (1761–1814), who produced a violin concerto and six string quartets, and Bernhard Henrik Crusell (1775–1838), a famous clarinettist. Fredrik Pacius (1809–1891), who was of German origin, was an important organizer of Helsinki's musical life. He composed the Finnish national anthem. Composer-pedagogue Martin Wegelius (1846–1906) and composer-conductor Robert Kajanus (1856–1933) preceded the greatest Finnish composer, Jean Sibelius (1865–1957). Sibelius began in the spirit of Finland's national epic, the Kalevala, and ended with universalism in the last of his seven symphonies. Erik Tawaststjerna (1916–) has won international fame, especially as a Sibelius researcher.

Erkki Melartin (1875–1937) and Toivo Kuula (1883–1918) are known above all for their vocal music;

The medieval Olavinlinna Castle in Savonlinna makes an imposing backdrop for the annual opera festival. A performance of Mozart's "Magic Flute" in summer, 1975.

Selim Palmgren (1878–1951), who reveals impressionistic traits, composed five piano concertos. Oskar Merikanto (1868–1924) gained popularity through his melodious songs and operas; his son Aarre Merikanto (1893–1958) was one of the first modernists in Finland and the first major performances in the 1960s and 1970s of his opera "Juha" (1920–1922) were momentous events. "Pohjalaisia" (The Ostrobothnians, 1924) by Leevi Madetoja (1887–1947) is traditionally regarded as Finland's national opera. Madetoja was also an important symphony composer. The Lied composer Yrjö Kilpinen (1892–1959) and Uuno Klami (1900–1961), a composer of orchestral works influenced by impressionism, were the first representatives of the musicworld appointed to the Academy of Finland. They were followed by Joonas Kokkonen (1921–), who composed the opera "Viimeiset kiusaukset" (The Last Temptations). The older men who have enriched Finnish music since the war include Erik Bergman (1911–), a unique proponent of the avant-garde and exotism, the opera and ballet composers Tauno Marttinen (1912–), Ahti Sonninen (1914–), and Tauno Pylkkänen (1918–1980), Bengt Johansson (1914–), who has developed choral expression, and symphony composer Einar Englund (1916–).

Wäinö Aaltonen, sculptor, painter.

The productive Einojuhani Rautavaara (1928–), who has worked in most spheres of music, Usko Meriläinen (1930–), composer of ballet music, Aulis Sallinen (1935–), who composed the operas "Ratsumies" (The Horseman) and "Punainen Viiva" (The Red Line), Erkki Salmenhaara (1941–), a music researcher and composer, Pehr-Henrik Nordgren (1944–), who shows a Japanese influence, Leif Segerstam (1944–), conductor-composer, and Kalevi Aho (1949–), who has already composed five symphonies, belong to the vanguard of innovative creators.

The main scenes for music performances are Finland's National Opera (f. 1911), Finlandia Hall (completed 1971), which is the centre of the Helsinki Festival, and the Savonlinna Opera Festival. The performing art of music has produced notable singers (Aino Ackté, Aulikki Rautavaara, Anita Välkki, Taru Valjakka, Irma Urrila, Kim Borg, Martti Talvela, Tom Krause, Pekka Nuotio, Jorma Hynninen and, most recently, Matti Kastu), conductors (in addition to those already mentioned, Georg Schnéevoigt, Paavo Berglund, Jorma Panula, Okko Kamu, Kari Tikka) and cellists (Arto Noras).

Light music is very popular. Jazz and pop music also have many competent representatives. There has been a fruitful interest in workers' music in recent years.

Eliel Saarinen, architect. His works established the national romantic school of architecture in Finland. Moved to the United States in 1923 where his functional buildings for the Cranbrook Foundation had a great influence on the country's architecture. His main creation in Finland is Helsinki Railway Station (1905–1914).

Finlandia Hall, made of white marble, is a concert and congress building in Helsinki. Designed by Alvar Aalto, it was completed in 1971. The heads of North American and European states convened here in 1975 for the Conference on Security and Cooperation in Europe. Behind, right, is the tower of the National Museum; on the left, in the background, is the Parliament Building.

Taivallahti Church (Timo and Tuomo Suomalainen, Helsinki 1969) represents modern Finnish church architecture at its boldest. The church is built of Finnish copper, glass, wood and granite inside natural rock; Finnish textiles were used for the interior decoration.

Architecture

The most important achievements of old Finnish architecture are the medieval castles and rough grey-stone churches, and the elaborate wooden churches with belfries created in the 18th century by the carpenter-masterbuilders who had risen from humble origins. The most important representative of the Neo-classical era was C.L. Engel (1778–1840), who created Helsinki's monumental, stylistically unusually harmonious centre in Empire style in the early 19th century. The turn of the century was dominated by National Romanticism, the stylistic ideals of which derived from Karelian wood architecture, the medieval grey-stone churches and the rich ornamentation of the European Art Nouveau. The great names of this period were Eliel Saarinen (1873–1950), Armas Gesellius (1874–1916), Armas Lindgren (1874–1929) and Lars Sonck (1870–1956), who designed both private houses and great monumental works. Eliel Saarinen moved to the United States in 1923, enriching its architecture with many prominent works. In the 1920s, the more severe forms of Classicism and more rational stylistic aspirations were adopted. This stylistic trend received its most monumental expression in the Parliament House designed by J.S. Sirén (1889–1961).

The breakthrough of Functionalism came at the end of the 1920s. The leading architects of the trend were Erik Bryggman (1891–1955) and Alvar Aalto (1898–1976), the greatest name in modern Finnish architecture, one of the best-known reformers of architecture in the world, whose influence covers broad areas: urban and regional planning, district plans, interior decoration and industrial art.

The effects of Finnish functionalism are reflected in both towns and rural districts, above all in rural industrial centres. It is a creative art that exploits the opportunities offered by industrialization and standardization. The result is healthier and more practical housing, schools, hospitals, industrial plants, office buildings. Their aesthetic values arise from the technical construction, not from ornamentation pasted on.

Among the most noted of the younger generation architects who have won considerable international recognition are Viljo Revell (1910–1964), Aulis Blomstedt (1906–1979), Aarne Ervi (1910–1977), Kaija (1920–) and Heikki (1918–) Siren, Aarno Ruusuvuori (1925–) and Reima Pietilä (1925–).

Alvar Aalto, architect, furniture designer, expert in town planning. Works: National Pensions Institute (1956), The House of Culture (1958), Finlandia Hall (1971), all in Helsinki, Jyväskylä University (1957). Abroad: Maison Carré in France (1958), Interbau block of apartments (Berlin 1957), Scandinavia House (Reykjavik 1968), Opera House in Essen (1971).

Akseli Gallen-Kallela: Lemmin-käinen's Mother, detail.

Akseli Gallen-Kallela, painter, graphic artist. Main works: Aino (1891), The Forming of the Sampo (1893), The Defence of the Sampo (1896), Lemmin-käinen's Mother and Revenge of Joukahainen (1897), all inspired by the Kalevala epic.

Painting

The oldest products of the art of painting are the murals in medieval churches (e.g. in the stone churches of Hattula and Lohja and in the Ostrobothnian wooden churches). The most famous church painters were Henricus Pictor in the 15th and Mikael Toppelius in the 18th century.

The Fine Arts Association of Finland (f. 1848) had a decisive influence on the development of Finnish art. A pioneering user of national sources, e.g. the Kalevala, was the romanticist R.W. Ekman (1803–1873). The paintings of Magnus (1805–1868) and Ferdinand (1822–1906) von Wright, known mainly as painters of animals, displayed the spirit of the Biedermeier style. The Düsseldorf School was represented by the first great name in landscape painting in Finland, Werner Holmberg (1830–1860).

The period of ascendancy, called the Golden Age of Finnish Art, began towards the end of the 19th century. It combined national romanticism and some of the forms of French naturalism and synthetism and Italian Early Renaissance. The list of well-known artists began with Albert Edelfelt (1854–1905), who, with his historical paintings, portrayal of the life of the people and portraits, introduced the new French art trends. The leading representative of national romanticism was Akseli Gallen-Kallela (1865–1931), the artist who had the broadest reach, the pioneer of our graphic and industrial arts. He created many masterpieces which were inspired by Finnish folk poetry and the scenery and people of the virgin wilds. Eero Järnefelt (1863–1937) was a refined depicter of the life of the people and a top-ranking portraitist. Pekka Halonen (1865–1933) painted both monumental compositions of people and delicate and refined landscapes.

Magnus Enckell (1873–1925) and Hugo Simberg (1873–1917) became the principal representatives of symbolism. Juho Rissanen (1873–1950), who belonged to the same generation and rose straight from humble origins, painted the life of the people with primitive force and simplicity. Early in the 20th century two art groups emerged whose aspirations were in many respects antithetical. The Septem group (f. 1912) headed by Magnus Enckell sought to introduce French post-impressionism and colorism into our art. The artists of the November group (f. 1917) were champions of the expressionistic trend. The leader of this group was Tyko Sallinen (1879–1955), one of the most unconventional exponents of Finnish art, who portrayed common men and women with a directly explosive force and brutality. Helene Schjerfbeck (1862–1946) may also be called an expressionist, but she was the very opposite of Sallinen: her later production in particular was extremely restrained, refined and of inner compulsion. The first

Unto Koistinen: Nude, 1968.

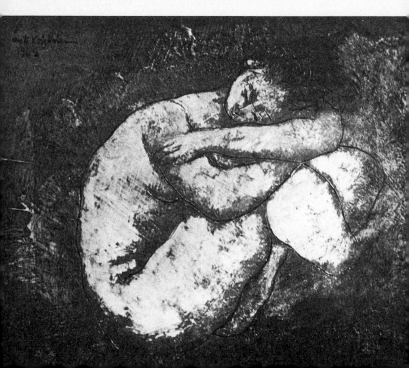

The Sibelius Monument in Helsinki is the creation of Eila Hiltunen, one of the most gifted sculptors in Finland. The monument consists of steel tubes welded together and a separate portrait relief. The monument weighs 24 tons and is approx. 10 m high.

naivists were Sulho Sipilä (1895–1949) and Vilho Lampi (1898–1936). They were most active in the 1930s when signs of surrealism began to appear. The spiritual heir of the November group was the October group (f. 1933). Its most prominent artist is Aimo Kanerva (1909–), who is known for his bold pictures of people and his refined landscapes in water colour. The portrayals of people and female motifs of Unto Koistinen (1917–) – who is also close to the October group – have a fantasy-like quality and expressiveness.

In the last couple of decades painting has continued to follow the international "isms" but without rejecting the specific national character. The paintings of Veikko Vionoja (1909–), who specialises in melancholy and heavy village scenes and interiors, and the post-cubistic works of Olli Miettinen (1899–1969) are characterised by a fresh Nordicism. An early exponent of concretism was Birger Carlstedt (1907–1975) and one of the leading painters of the trend today is Sam Vanni (1908–). Among the numerous abstract painters may be mentioned Per Stenius (1922–) and Anitra Lucander (1918–). Leading exponents of surrealism are Alpo Jaakola (1929–) and Juhani Linnovaara (1934–), both of whom are sculptors as well.

Sculpture

Relatively little has been preserved of the production of early Finnish sculptors. The most valuable part of the wooden sculptures in medieval churches consisted of imported works, chiefly from Germany and the Netherlands. The "Master of Lieto" was the best-known of Finland's medieval sculptors.

Pioneers of the art of sculpture were Erik Cainberg (1771—1816), the first to treat a Kalevala motif in pictorial form, and Carl Eneas Sjöstrand (1823—1909), whose realistic productions had a wakening impact on Finland's young art of sculpture. Classicism was represented by Walter Runeberg (1838—1920), whose main works include the monument to J.L. Runeberg in the Esplanade park in Helsinki (1885) and the monument to Czar Alexander II in Helsinki's Senate Square (1894). A rare natural talent was Johannes Takanen (1849—1885), whose works, especially his female and child figures, were characterised by plasticity and a natural grace. Robert Stigell (1852—1907) favoured realism and the baroque; his best-known creation is the powerful "The Shipwrecked" on Observatory Hill in Helsinki (1898). One of the most spirited and central personalities of his time was Ville Vallgren (1855—1940), whose production comprises both great public statues and small graceful pieces in Art Nouveau style made of fired clay. His best-loved sculpture is the Havis Amanda fountain in Helsinki's Market Square (1908).

Baby's Chair No. 02 728 97, a socially critical sculpture by Rauni Liukko, portrays the subordinate position of the child in the mechanized and cold world.

The outstanding figure of Finland's newer sculpture was doubtless Wäinö Aaltonen (1894—1966). He used

Although industrial art is centralized in large factories, both traditional and modern objects d'art and utility articles are produced in private workshops as a counterbalance to mass production.

Furniture designed by Alvar Aalto in the 1930s is already classical. This chair is of bent plywood; the seat is of saddle strapping. The four-part table is of birch, the lamp of painted aluminium. Artek.

bronze, ceramic and marble, but above all granite, as his material, and was the first to use granite since the old Egyptians. Two typical features of Aaltonen's style are a powerful monumental form, depending on the nature of his material, and unadorned lyricism. His main works are the monument to Aleksis Kivi in the Railway Square in Helsinki (1939), the four sculptures on Hämeensilta Bridge in Tampere (1929) and the statue of Paavo Nurmi (1924). Aimo Tukiainen (1917–) has made monumental and portrait sculptures. His style was figurative to begin with, later abstract. His monumental works include numerous memorials to war heroes and, his main work, the equestrian statue of Marshal Mannerheim in Helsinki (1960).

Finland's present-day sculptural art is dominated by many strong female sculptors: Eila Hiltunen (1922–) shows an original and bold imagination and versatile technical ability. She specialises in the welding technique, e.g. fountains in Tampere and Helsinki and the Sibelius monument in Helsinki (1963–1967). Laila Pullinen (1937–) expresses classical ideals of beauty. She has gained international fame with her bronze and copper sculpture made by the blasting technique. Eeva Ryynänen (1915–) uses wood and gives it life in her magnificently realised human and animal figures and reliefs. One of the most notable of the young sculptresses is Rauni Liukko (1940–): her art is participatory and subjective; working women are frequent motifs of her works, and quite particularly small children fettered by a violent and confining society.

Several other modern Finnish sculptors take a critical sociological attitude, e.g. Ossi Somma (1926–), Kimmo Kaivanto (1932–) and Kimmo Pyykkö (1940–).

Industrial Art

The debut of Finnish industrial art abroad took place at the World Exhibition in Paris in 1900. The outstanding industrial artists of the period were Akseli Gallen-Kallela, Louis Sparre and A.W. Finch of the Iris Factory in Porvoo (1897–1902), and the architects Eliel Saarinen and Armas Lindgren. Their legacy lives on. Finnish industrial art has gained world renown and harvested numerous prizes at international exhibitions and competitions.

To generalise, Finnish industrial art is characterised by very simple, clear-cut form-giving or an eastern-influenced ornamentalism and glow of colours. The wooden furniture designed by Alvar Aalto is already classical. Other furniture designers are Ilmari Tapiovaara, Yrjö Kukkapuro, Eero Aarnio and Antti Nurmesniemi, who is known also as an interior architect and designer of household utensils and lamps. Tapio Wirkkala, Kaj Franck, Timo Sarpaneva and Oiva Toikka are versatile artists who have designed both household utensils, glass and utility ware. Ceramic is the raw material of Rut Bryk, Kyllikki Salmenhaara (1915–1981), Toini Muona, Raija Tuumi, Friedl Kjellberg, Heljä Liukko-Sundström and Birger Kaipiainen, whereas Kaija Aarikka works in wood. Lisa Johansson-Pape, Paavo and Helena Tynell and Yki Nummi design lamps, Bertel Gardberg and Björn Weckström jewellery, Maija Isola and Vuokko Eskolin printed fabrics – Eskolin dresses as well. Marimekko Oy has acquired international renown in the printed textile branch. Marjatta Metsovaara, Dora Jung and Elsa Montell-Saanio, who has revived the Lapp "raanu" (counterpane) tradition, specialise in decorative textiles. The many gifted artists of Suomen Käsityön Ystävät Oy

Finnish ballet is full of vigour and has given the world many artists of top international class. The eminent prima ballerina Marianne Rumjantseva partnered by Aku Ahjolinna in Swan Lake.

(Friends of Finnish Handicrafts, f. 1879) have revived the old popular handicraft tradition for various textiles. Ritva Puotila is a well-known designer of "ryijy» tapestries.

Theatre and Film

The great popularity of dramatic art and amateur dramatics in Finland has its roots in the national character and customs of the people. The oldest form of theatre was the school plays performed after the Reformation. It was not until the beginning of the 19th century that the first theatres were built. The first Finnish-language play was "Silmänkääntäjä" (The Conjurer) by Pietari Hannikainen, which had its premiere in 1847. However, the performance of Aleksis

Kivi's "Lea" in 1869 in Helsinki is regarded as the beginning of Finnish-language dramatic art. The Finnish Theatre was founded in 1872. Amateur dramatics are still very much alive.

There are 42 professional theatres in Finland. There are, in addition, a great many semi-professional and amateur theatres, summer theatres, student and youth theatres. The radio theatre, the TV and the commercial TV theatres are of country-wide importance. In the number of theatres and the size of audiences Finland is one of the leading countries in Europe. There is a considerable exchange of visits with foreign theatres. Of the many talented Finnish directors the best known in Scandinavia are Vivica Bandler, Lasse Pöysti, Ralf Långbacka, Jack Witikka and Kalle Holmberg.

The theatre organization as a whole is currently undergoing a change with the aim of establishing a statutory regional theatre system. Touring professional groups are a new phenomenon, which fills the gap left by the established theatres. Their status is still vague and awaits organization.

In the 1978—1979, season State-subsidised theatres gave 10,470 performances, which drew an attendance of 2,652,000.

The Finnish film industry, which began in 1919 produces almost exclusively for the Finnish market. Seven feature films were made in 1979. There are 317 cinemas with 91,098 seats in all. Between the arrival of the sound film and the 1960s numerous films were produced, but then came a decline which has persisted ever since. However, there have been a couple of important artistic successes in recent years, such as "The Earth is a Sinful Song", directed by Rauni Mollberg, which has won fame abroad. Mikko Niskanen is a director who has social productions with a strong message to his credit.

Radio and Press

Broadcasting is the monopoly of Oy Yleisradio Ab, the Finnish Broadcasting Company, 93 % of whose shares are owned by the State. Broadcasting is financed with funds from television licences collected annually. No radio licence is needed. A total of 10,600 hours of Finnish radio broadcasts are sent each year, while there are 4,600 hours of Swedish broadcasts. Music accounts for 50 % of the broadcast time.

After test transmissions beginning in 1956, the Finnish Broadcasting Company started regular television broadcasts in 1958. By the end of 1980 there were 752,200 licences for black and white TV sets and 786,000 licences for colour sets.

The first newspaper to be published in Finland was printed in Swedish and appeared in 1771; the first in Finnish appeared five years later.

Finland has 55 newspapers published at least 4 times a week. Eight of these are in Swedish. The biggest newspapers are Helsingin Sanomat, independent (Helsinki, circulation 392,800), Aamulehti, National Coalition (Tampere 133,400), Turun Sanomat, independent (Turku 130,200), Maaseudun Tulevaisuus, independent, 3 times a week (Helsinki, 126,300), Iltasanomat is an afternoon paper (Helsinki, 121,500). The biggest Swedish newspaper is Hufvudstadsbladet (Helsinki, 63,900). The largest newspaper of the Finnish People's Democratic League is Kansan Uutiset (Helsinki, 56,700). The largest Social Democratic Party newspaper is Suomen Sosialidemokraatti (Helsinki, 42,700).

Some 1,500 periodicals are published in Finland annually. Those with the largest circulation are Apu (weekly, 302,900), Seura (weekly, 276,600) and Valitut Palat (Reader's Digest, Finnish edition, monthly, 270,000). The largest women's magazines are Kotiliesi (bimonthly, 214,000), Kodin Kuvalehti (bimonthly, 183,800), and Jaana (weekly, 128,500).

SPORT

The Finnish sports have long been skiing, rowing, running, wrestling and ball games. Organised sport gained momentum in the 1870s. Finland won its first Olympic gold medals in wrestling and the discus in the 1906 interim Games. In 1912, the country made a spectacular breakthrough in Stockholm: 9 gold medals, 6 in track and field and 3 for wrestling. Hannes Kolehmainen, the distance runner, won 3 of them. Finnish successes in the Olympic arena continued in the 20s and 30s, with the biggest names being Paavo Nurmi, who won a total of 9 gold medals, and Ville Ritola, who

Pesäpallo – a modified form of baseball – is the national game of the Finns. It is played with enthusiasm from a very early age.

won 5 gold medals. The greatest name of recent time has been Lasse Viren, who took 2 gold medals in track events in both the 1972 Munich Games and the 1976 Montreal Games.

Starting with Julius Saaristo in the 1910s and 1920s Finnish javelin throwers leaped into prominence, producing such names as Jonni Myyrä, Matti Järvinen, Tapio Rautavaara, Pauli Nevala and Hannu Siitonen.

Because of the natural conditions, winter sports have a firmly established position in Finland. Big international winter sports meets are held every year at Lahti, Puijo (Kuopio), Ounasvaara (Rovaniemi) and Ruka (Kuusamo). The cross-country skiers have brought home an abundant harvest of Olympic medals and world championships: Veli Saarinen, Veikko Hakulinen, Kalevi Hämäläinen, Eero Mäntyranta, Juha Mieto, and, among the ladies, Lydia Wideman, Marjatta Kajosmaa, Helena Takalo and Hilkka Riihivuori. Finnish ski

After already winning a gold medal in the 10,000 metres at the Montreal Olympics, 1976, Finnish runner Lasse Viren came first in the 5,000 metres, too. This made him the first runner ever to win both the 5,000 and 10,000 metres in two successive Olympics, since he had performed the same feat in Munich, in 1972.

jumpers have also sailed into headlines from time to time, men such as Antti Hyvärinen, Veikko Kankkonen and Jouko Törmänen. In speed skating Clas Thunberg in the 1920s took many Olympic golds and world championships, and more recently our woman skater Kaija Mustonen won an Olympic gold in 1968.

Finland has also gained a fine reputation in gymnastics (4 gold medals in 1948). Heikki Savolainen won Olympic medals from 1928 right up to 1952. The first Finnish boxer to win a gold was Sten Suvio, in 1936. Sculling was Finland's strong event at the Helsinki Olympics in 1952 (4 golds). Pentti Linnosvuo put Finland on the shooting map in 1956 and 1964, and Kaarlo Kangasniemi brought home gold in weightlifting from the 1968 Games. Pertti Karppinen brought Finland its first gold medal in rowing in 1976 and won first place again in 1980. Finland also received its first Olympic victories in archery (18-year-old Tomi Poikolainen – Finland's youngest Olympic winner ever) and sailing (Esko Rechardt) at the 1980 Games.

Paavo Nurmi (1897–1973), champion middle- and long-distance runner during the 1920s. Won 9 Olympic gold and 3 silver medals. Held 24 official world records for distances ranging from the mile to the marathon.

From 1906 to 1980 the Finns have won a total of 120 gold medals, 112 silver medals and 130 bronze medals or 362 medals in all at the summer and winter Olympics.

In recent years Finland has produced some top-flight bowlers – of both sexes – and some of the world's best women orienteers (Liisa Veijalainen, Outi Borgenström).

Finland has also had some of the top names in motorcycle racing. Jarno Saarinen won the road racing world championship in 1972, Heikki Mikkola won four motocross world championships in 1974–78 and Yrjö Vesterinen won three trial world championships in 1976–78. Our rally drivers are world famous – Timo Mäkinen, Rauno Aaltonen, Pauli Toivonen, Simo Lampinen, Hannu Mikkola, Markku Alén, Ari Vatanen.

There is also a notable interest in sport for the sake of just keeping fit rather than striving for top competition honours. Thousands of citizens of all ages are to be found on the ski tracks, forest paths and sports grounds, in swimming baths, gymnasia and physical fitness schools, in search of health, beauty and fun. A great advocate of national physical fitness has been Professor Lauri (Tahko) Pihkala (1888–1981).

The two main central sports federations are: the Finnish Central Sports Federation (SVUL) and the Workers' Sports Federation (TUL). The former manages most international contacts and competitions. The latter can record excellent results (106 wins) from the Workers' Olympics of the 1920s and 1930s.

Most of the financial backing for sport in Finland comes from the proceeds of the State-run football pools and other betting events. Instruction and research in physical training are concentrated in the universities of

Jyväskylä and Turku, the Finnish Sports Institute at Vierumäki, and the Pajulahti and Vuokatti Sports Institutes, among others.

The Tourist Season

Finland is one of the largest — and smallest — countries
in Europe: large in size, small in population. The
distance between the southernmost point in Finland and
the northernmost is over 1000 km (720 miles), so that
there are great differences not only in landscape but also
in climate. In Lapland the midnight sun shines night and
day for the whole of June and part of July. In southern
Finland spring comes earlier and summer lasts longer.
At Midsummer there is as much as 19 hours of daylight.

Most foreigners visit Finland during the summer
months; in July the mean temperature in southern
Finland is the same as in the Netherlands, Belgium and
England (16 ° to 18 °C). The autumn offers bright
colours, especially in Lapland. In winter there are
cultural events and excellent opportunities for
cross-country skiing, with the season lasting in southern
Finland from January to the end of March, and in
Lapland, in brilliant sunshine, until early May.

What Finland Can Offer the Tourist

Finland offers the tourist abundant space, peace and
pure air. Vast forests are broken up by lakes and laced
with rivers. Tens of thousands of islands dot the 60,000
lakes and the sea, especially in the south and south-west
where the Baltic washes through the archipelagoes to
the coast. And in the north Finnish Lapland all but
touches the Arctic Ocean.

The Finns are never happier than when they can
escape from the sophistication of town life to the rural
environment of a holiday home on a lake shore or river
bank. Here is true freedom: to swim, sunbathe, fish, row,
sail or canoe, to walk through the forests, or simply do
nothing at all. And visitors can do just the same when
staying at a holiday village, a remote log cabin, a
farmhouse or a camping site; nearly all are located by a
lake, river or the sea.

From June to August, the lakeland maze is
crisscrossed by regular boat routes, some maintained by
the romantic old steamers, others by modern motor
vessels or a hydrofoil. On some of these routes you can
travel for several days, sleeping and eating on board, or
stopping off to pick up another boat the next day.

Finnish travel agencies arrange guided and
independent tours, especially to the lake district and
Lapland.

Finland's coastal archipelago of over 30,000 islands and skerries is one of the most beautiful in the world. On the north-east coast of the Gulf of Finland, close to the town of Kotka, is the beautiful island of Kaunissaari, whose inhabitants live mostly by fishing. Its fine sand beaches and unique rustic culture make the island a popular tourist spot.

But Finland is indeed a modern country in architecture and design. Alvar Aalto's work is seen all over the country, from Finlandia Hall in Helsinki to Lappia Hall in Rovaniemi. There are also medieval churches and castles, the neo-classical centre of Helsinki, small idyllic wooden towns and old rural culture.

In the regions close to the Soviet border, one can also sense the impact of culture from the east. Cultural influences from the west and the east once met here; Kuopio's Orthodox museum, with its collection of icons, and Greek Orthodox church festivities are well worth seeing.

Modern tourist hotels have been built all over the country. In summer it is possible to rent a cottage. There are about 5,600 privately owned holiday cabins ranging from the humblest fishing hut on the coast or in the archipelago to luxury log villas on the lakes. All the cabins are furnished, and cooking utensils and crockery are included as well as fuel for heating, cooking and lighting, and usually a sauna and a boat.

The lakes are ideal for canoeing, and guided trips are arranged in central and eastern Finland and in Lapland.

On Saimaa there are 2,000 km (1,250 miles) of marked routes.

Hiking is both for the Sunday walker and the experienced hiker willing to take on the rugged wilderness, and there are many marked trails.

Cycling tours are becoming increasingly popular and there are a number of planned routes available. Tourists can also enter the 230-mile Finn Cycling Tour.

Finland is also good for fishing. Pike, perch, whitefish, grayling, brown trout, pike-perch, bream and burbot are found in Finland. Some of these fish, together with salmon, trout, cod and flounder, can be caught in the Gulf of Finland and the Gulf of Bothnia.

Rovaniemi on the Arctic Circle can be reached by plane in 1 hour 10 minutes from Helsinki. From Lapland it is possible to visit North Cape in Norway. From Helsinki there are excursions by Russian ship, bus, train or plane to Leningrad, and there is also a ferry to Tallinn, Estonia, on the other side of the Gulf of Finland.

In winter there is of course skiing. You can take part in a guided cross-country skiing tour or a reindeer safari in Lapland. There are many national and international skiing competitions at Lahti, Kuusamo, Kuopio and Rovaniemi. Anyone can take part in the cross-country competitions such as the Finlandia Ski Race (75 km), Pirkka Skiing (91 km), Oulu Terva Skiing (75 km) and Arctic Circle Skiing (65 km).

Vuokatti, formed by high wooded hills, is a popular holiday and winter sports centre in Sotkamo, amidst the most magnificent scenery in Finland.

The winter tourist can choose between centres such as Laajavuori, outside Jyväskylä, and Lahti (site of the World Skiing Championship in 1978) in southern Finland, or visit one of the many skiing resorts in Lapland.

Finland has become an important venue for conferences in recent years and provides a fresh alternative for organizers of international congresses. Helsinki, Espoo and Turku are the biggest congress centres at the moment, but many other places also offer high-standard facilities for international meetings. Over 150 international conferences and congresses are held in Finland each year, with the number of participants exceeding 30,000. Around one-third of Finland's conference guests come from Scandinavia, the other two-thirds representing a wide range of nationalities.

Festivals

There are quite a number of festivals during the summer months, when the regular theatres and concert halls are closed. The events range from folk dances and music, local market days, cultural events, and outdoor art exhibitions, to regattas and lumberjack games and gold-panning championships. Finland Festivals comprise the following cultural events:

- Kuopio Dance and Music Festival, classical ballet, modern dance, seminars and brass band music
- Helsinki Festival, concerts, opera, ballet and drama
- Jyväskylä Arts Festival, varied programme, including lectures and seminars on music, drama, dance and film
- Savonlinna Opera Festival, opera performances, concerts and art exhibitions, etc.
- Pori International Jazz Festival, jazz concerts and jam sessions
- Kaustinen Folk Music Festival
- Turku Music Festival, chamber music, opera and choral music
- The Tampere Theatre Summer, special theatre performances
- Naantali Music Festival, chamber music, concerts, Finnish and foreign soloists
- Lahti International Organ Festival, concerts, Finnish and foreign organists, concert by yearly winner of national organ competition, choral concerts, courses, exhibitions.

It is advisable to make hotel reservations in good time. Tickets for the Savonlinna Opera Festival, in particular, should be ordered in advance.

In addition to these big festivals, hundreds of other events concerning Finland's cultural and national heritage are arranged every year. Further information

can be obtained from Finland Festivals, Simonkatu 12 B 15, 00100 Helsinki 10.

Routes to Finland

Air: Finnair and many other international airlines such as Acroflot, Air France, Austrian Airlines, British Airways, CSA, KLM, Lufthansa, LOT, Malev and SAS have regular connections to Finland from New York and all major European cities such as London, Paris, Zürich, Frankfurt, Amsterdam, Hamburg, Brussels, Madrid, Rome, Vienna, Oslo, Copenhagen and Stockholm. Finnair flies DC-10 and DC-8 jets on the Atlantic route.

Sea: Finland can be reached by Finnlines' modern car ferries. The direct route from Travemünde in the Federal Republic of Germany is operated with the Finnjet'', the world's largest car ferry. The Finnjet'' has a cruising speed of 30 knots and reaches Helsinki in 22 hours.

Tallinn and Leningrad (cruise) can be reached by sea from Helsinki.

Between Sweden and Finland there are dozens of daily car ferry connections; Silja Line and Viking Line ply the routes from Stockholm to Helsinki, Turku and Naantali. Some of the ships also call at Mariehamn in the Åland Islands. In the Gulf of Bothnia there are car ferry

Among the most charming places in Finnish towns are the markets, where fish, fruit, berries, vegetables, flowers, handicraft products, household utensils, and even cheap clothes are sold in the mornings. The market place in Hamina.

connections from Umeå and Sundsvall in Sweden to Vaasa in Finland, and from Skellefteå to Pietarsaari.

Land: There are rail connections between Finland and the USSR with direct trains from Moscow and Leningrad, and from Sweden at the northern border. Motorists can use the car ferries or drive through Sweden or Norway or through several border crossing points on the frontier.

Passports and Visas

No passport is required of citizens of the Scandinavian countries. In addition, a British Visitor's Passport, intended for a tourist trip lasting not more than 3 months, is accepted as a passport. On the same conditions certificates of identification issued by the officials of Austria, Belgium, Liechtenstein, France, the Federal Republic of Germany and Switzerland are accepted. No visa is required from citizens of most countries of the world.

Customs Regulations

In addition to personal effects intended for use during the journey and foodstuffs for consumption during the journey travellers resident abroad may bring into Finland, duty-free, goods up to the value of 500 Fmk or, if the traveller is under 16, to the value of 250 Fmk. This amount may not include more than 15 kg (c. 33 lb.) of foodstuffs, of which 5 kg (c. 11 lb.) at most may be edible fats. However, it is forbidden to import more than 2.5 kg (c. 5 lb.) of butter.

In addition to the above allowances, travellers may also bring in the following maximum amounts:
a) 200 cigarettes or 250 g (1/2 lb) of other manufactured tobacco;
b) in the case of travellers residing outside Europe: 400 cigarettes or 500 g (1 lb) of other manufactured tobacco;
c) alcoholic beverages as follows: travellers aged 20 or over: either 2 l of beer, 1 l of other mild alcoholic beverages and 1 l of other alcoholic beverages, or 2 l of beer and 2 l of other mild alcoholic beverages. Travellers aged 18 or over: 2 l of beer and 2 l of other mild alcoholic beverages.

Strong spirits may only be brought in by persons aged 20 years or over, mild alcoholic beverages by persons aged 18 years or over, and manufactured tobacco by persons aged 16 years or over.

A traveller not residing in Finland may bring in unlimited amounts of Finnish and foreign currency.
– Foreign currency may be exchanged at all banks and

authorized exchange centres, such as travel agencies, hotels, etc.

A person resident abroad can take out of Finland the currencies he brought in.

A detailed customs guide for travellers published by the Finnish customs authorities is available on ships serving Finland and in Finnish Tourist Board offices abroad.

Motor vehicles can be brought into the country for the tourist's own use for a maximum of one year against a driver's licence and green card. Otherwise import duty and taxes are collected or surety to be returned when the vehicle is taken out of the country must be provided.

The best way of seeing Finland's unique lake scenery is to go on a cruise on one of the inland waterways. Lake Päijänne in Central Finland.

Travel in Finland

Air: Finland has one of the densest and cheapest air networks in Europe. The northernmost of the 17 airports in the country is about 200 km (125 miles) north of the Arctic Circle. Flying the length of Finland is the best way to appreciate Finland's thousands of lakes and its vast forests. Most Finnair domestic services use DC-9 jets, the others using Super Caravelle jets or Convair Metropolitan aircraft. The flight from Helsinki to Rovaniemi on the Arctic Circle is about 1 hour 10 minutes.

The Finnair Holiday Ticket fare, $180, entitles the

bearer to 15 days of unlimited air travel in Finland. The
Holiday Ticket is available to any permanent resident of
countries outside Scandinavia. Midnight Sun Flights
with a special programme are operated in the summer.

Railways: Finland has nearly 6,000 km of track, and
rail travel is relatively inexpensive.

The Tourist Ticket is valid throughout the year and
includes travel by rail, bus, boat and air. The Finnrail
Pass allows unlimited travel throughout Finland for a
certain period. A pass valid for 15 days in 2nd class costs
$88. For young people under 26 years the Interrail Pass
is the best bargain.

Bus and Coach Services: There is a good coach
network all over Finland, and this is the only means of
overland travel in Lapland, since there is no railway
north of Kemijärvi.

Motoring: Tourists who wish to motor in Finland may
either bring their own car (see Customs Regulations) or
hire one with or without a driver. Information on
motoring in Finland can be obtained from the Finnish
Automobile and Touring Club, Kansakoulukatu 10,
00100 Helsinki 10.

Steamer traffic: Steamer services are maintained
along the coasts and on the inland waterways. Modern
water buses maintain regular services on the main
tourist routes.

Useful brochures: Finland Travel Facts. Hotels,
Motels, Hostels. Camping Sites and Youth Hostels.
Finnish Lapland. Brochures on various regions and
towns in Finland also available. Free booklets and
brochures can be obtained from Finnish Tourist Board
offices and travel agencies.

Hotels

The price level varies from district to district. In
Helsinki, a single room in a 1st class hotel costs Fmk
180–250, a double room Fmk 250–350. A single room
in a summer hotel" costs Fmk 80–150 and a double
room Fmk 140–200. The summer hotels" are student
residences of a high standard. They are available in
Finnish university towns: Helsinki, Turku, Tampere,
Oulu, Jyväskylä and Rovaniemi.

First class hotels are to be found in all important towns
and in tourist centres, especially in the lake district and
Lapland.

THE FINNISH NATIONAL ANTHEM

Our Land
Words J.L. Runeberg 1846
Translation by Clement Burbank Shaw

Music by Fredrik Pacius 1848

1. Our land, our land, our fatherland, Sound loud, O name of worth!
2. Thy blossom, in the bud laid low, Yet ripened shall upspring.

No mount that meets the heaven's band, No hidden vale, no wave-
washed strand

See! From our love once more shall grow Thy light, thy joy, thy
hope, thy glow!

Is loved, as is our native North, Our own forefathers' earth.
And clearer yet one day shall ring The song our land shall sing.

WHO'S WHO

Paavo Berglund

Berglund, Paavo (b. 14.4.1929), conductor. Conductor for the Radio Symphony Orchestra 1955–62, senior conductor for the Radio Symphony Orchestra 1962–71, senior conductor for the Bournemouth Symphony Orchestra 1972–79, director of the Helsinki Philharmonic Orchestra 1975–79.

Bergman, Erik (b. 24.11.1911), composer and choral director. Professor of composition at the Sibelius Academy 1963–76. Compositions: Burla, Tre aspetti d'una serie dodecafonica, Aubade, Simbolo, Circulus and Colori ed improvisazioni for orchestra, Rubaiyat for a male-voice choir, baritone and orchestra, Aton for baritone, reciter, mixed choir and orchestra, Bauta for baritone, male choir and percussion, Sela for baritone, mixed choir and chamber orchestra, compositions for the organ, songs for orchestra, works for a male-voice choir and instrumental orchestras.

Erik Bergman

Haavikko, Paavo (b. 25.1.1931), author. Since 1967 he has been literary director of the Otava Publishing Company. Haavikko has published collections of poetry, plays and radio plays, novels and a collection of short stories. His works have been translated into several languages. Works published in English: Selected Poems, the short story Before History Begins, and the libretto for the opera The Horseman. In 1977 he published an important book on Finnish history in this century.

Paavo Haavikko

Haavisto, Heikki (b. 20.8.1935), agronomist. General secretary of the Central Union of Agricultural Producers 1966–67, managing director 1967–74 and chairman of the board since 1975.

Heikki Haavisto

Hiltunen, Eila (b. 22.11.1922), sculptress, professor. Her early sculptures depicting people were succeeded by an experimental period in the 1960s when she introduced welding techniques into sculpture. Her main work, the Sibelius Monument (Helsinki, 1967), is made of welded steel pipes. Her other works include People in the Procession of Time (Helsinki Town Hall, 1971), the Flame of Life (Tampere, 1972), the Palm Grove monument (Teheran, 1975), the Flame of Life II (Jeddah, 1979) and Copper Construction (Jeddah, 1980).

Eila Hiltunen

Jaakko Hintikka

Hintikka, Jaakko (b. 12.1.1929), philosopher, logician. Professor of practical philosophy at the University of Helsinki 1959–70, research professor for the Academy of Finland 1970–81, professor at Stanford University 1964–81 and Florida State University since 1978. He has achieved an internationally respected position as a leading representative of analytical philosophy and has published the following works, among others: Selected Essays (1969), Logic, Language-Games, and Information (1973), Time and Necessity: Studies in Aristotle's Theory of Modality (1973) and The Intentions of Intentionality and Other New Models for Modalities (1975).

Jorma Hynninen

Hynninen, Jorma (b. 3.4.1941), opera singer. Soloist for the Finnish National Opera since 1970. Lied concerts in London, West Berlin, Cologne, Budapest, Amsterdam, Stockholm, New York etc. Guest performances at La Scala, at the Vienna, Hamburg and Bavarian state operas, at the Paris Opera, at the Madrid and Savonlinna opera festivals etc.

Jaakko Ihamuotila

Ihamuotila, Jaakko (b. 15.11.1939), managing director and director of the board of the state oil company Neste Oy since 1980. Valmet Oy's planning director 1972–73 and managing director 1973–79. Member of Neste board of directors 1979.

Ilaskivi, Raimo (b. 26.5.1928), politician, Mayor of Helsinki since 1979. Managing director of the Finnish Bankers' Association 1961–79, manager of the Helsinki stock exchange 1964–79. Member of Parliament 1962–75.

Itälä, Jaakko (b. 7.5.1933), chairman of the Liberal Party of Finland since 1978. Managing director of the Mannerheim League for Child Welfare since 1968. Minister of Education 1970–71 and 1978–79.

Raimo Ilaskivi

Jakobson, Max (b. 30.9.1923), managing director of the Council of Economic Organisations of Finland, diplomat, author, permanent representative of Finland at the United Nations 1965–72, Finnish Ambassador to Sweden 1972–75. His publications include The Diplomacy of the Winter War (1961), and Finnish Neutrality (1968).

Jaakko Itälä

Jansson, Jan-Magnus (b. 24.1.1922), politician, scientist, editor-in-chief of Hufvudstadsbladet (Swedish-language newspaper in Helsinki) since 1974. Professor of political science at the University of Helsinki 1954–74. Chairman of the Paasikivi Society 1964–66 and since 1975, chairman of the Swedish

Max Jakobson

Jan-Magnus Jansson

Tove Jansson

Mikko Juva

People's Party 1966—73. Minister of Trade and Industry 1973—74.

Jansson, Tove (b. 9.8.1914), authoress, painter. Gained world fame as the creator of the Moomin characters. Her works have been translated into many languages. She was awarded the Hans Christian Andersen Prize in 1966.

Okko Kamu

Juva, Mikko (b. 22.11.1918), Archbishop of the Evangelical-Lutheran Church of Finland since 1978, historian, doctor of philosophy and theology. Professor of Finnish history at the University of Turku 1957—62, professor of Finnish and Scandinavian church history at the University of Helsinki 1962—78, Assistant Rector 1968—71, Rector 1971—73 and Chancellor 1973—78. Member of parliament 1964—66, chairman of the Liberal Party 1965—68. President of the Lutheran World Federation 1970—77.

Ahti Karjalainen

Kamu, Okko (b. 7.3.1946), conductor. First prize at a conducting competition arranged by the Herbert von Karajan Foundation in Berlin in 1969. First violin at the Finnish National Opera 1966—68, visiting conductor at the Royal Opera in Stockholm 1969—70, conductor at the Finnish Broadcasting Company 1970—72, senior conductor 1972—77, temporary professor of orchestral conducting at the Sibelius Academy 1971—72, visiting principal conductor of the Norrköping Symphony Orchestra 1972—78, senior conductor of the Oslo Philharmonic Orchestra 1975—79. Artistic director of the Helsinki Philharmonic Orchestra since 1981.

Urho Kekkonen

Karjalainen, Ahti (b. 10.2.1923), Centre Party politician, bank director, Ph.D. (political science). Member of the board of the Bank of Finland since 1958. Member of Parliament 1966—79 (Centre Party), deputy Minister of Finance 1957 and 1958, Minister of Trade and Industry 1959—61, Minister for Foreign Affairs 1961—62, 1964—70 and 1972—75, Prime Minister 1962—63 and 1970—71, Minister for Economy and of

Sakari Kiuru

Harry Kivijärvi

Kalevi Kivistö

Mauno Koivisto

Joonas Kokkonen

Erkki Laurila

the Cabinet Office 1976—77. Chairman of several trade delegations. Led the negotiations on Finnish association with EFTA. Host to the first stage of the Conference on Security and Cooperation in Europe in Helsinki.

Kekkonen, Urho (b. 3.9.1900), President of the Republic 1956—82. Member of the Board of Governors of the Bank of Finland 1946—56, Member of Parliament 1936—56, Minister of Justice and Assistant Minister of the Interior 1936—37, Minister of the Interior 1937—39, Minister of Justice 1944—46, Prime Minister and Minister of the Interior 1950—51, Prime Minister 1951—52, 1953, 1954—56, Prime Minister and Minister for Foreign Affairs 1952—53, Minister for Foreign Affairs 1954. Kekkonen was elected President of the Republic for the first time in 1956, the second time in 1962, the third time in 1968, and in 1973 his term in office was extended from 1974 to 1978. In 1978 he was re-elected President for the six-year period 1978—84. In autumn 1981 he gave notice that he was unable to continue serving as President because of illness. His term of office will officially end in 1982 when a new President has been elected.

Kekkonen has actively and successfully strengthened Finland's international position, and as Paasikivi's successor increased the mutual understanding between Finland and the Soviet Union. He proposed the formation of a nuclear-free zone in Scandinavia. On his initiative, Finland offered to host the Conference on Security and Cooperation in Europe in 1969. The final stage of this Conference took place in Helsinki in 1975.

Kiuru, Sakari (b. 18.4.1926), managing director of the Finnish Broadcasting Company since 1980. Director of TV 1 1975—79. Chairman of the Finnish National Commission for Unesco since 1972, chairman of Nordvision 1976—78.

Kivijärvi, Harry (b. 25.7.1931), sculptor. Specialized in stone in the 1960s. Has created several works in bronze, but has concentrated mainly on the use of black granite. His public works include the J.K. Paasikivi monument in Helsinki (1980).

Kivistö, Kalevi (b. 25.3.1941), chairman of the Finnish People's Democratic League since 1979. Minister at the Ministry of Education 1975—76 and and since 1977. Member of Parliament since 1972.

Koivisto, Mauno (b. 25.11.1923), Social Democratic politician, bank manager, Ph.D. Governor of the Bank of Finland since 1968, Minister of Finance 1966—67 and 1972, Prime Minister 1968—70 and since 1979.

Kokkonen, Joonas (b. 13.11.1923), composer. Professor of composition at the Sibelius Academy 1959–63, member of the Finnish Academy since 1963, member of the European Academy of the Sciences, Arts and Letters since 1981. Compositions include 4 symphonies, Sinfonia da camera for 12 stringed instruments, Music for strings, Inauguratio for orchestra, a cello concerto, 2 string quartets, a piano quintet and trio, a wind quintet, a cello sonata, the mass Missa a cappella for six-part mixed choir, Laudatio domini for mixed choir, the song cycles Tuonela of the Birds, Evenings and Sub rosa, and the opera The Last Temptations.

Risto Leskinen

Laurila, Erkki (b. 20.8.1913), physicist, professor of theoretical physics at Helsinki University of Technology 1945–63, member of the Academy of Finland since 1963, chairman of the Council of Nuclear Energy 1958–75, member of the board of the International Atomic Energy Agency 1960–61, 1964–65, 1968–69 and 1972–73. Constructed several measuring and control devices and developed magnetic methods for separating ores.

Väinö Linna

Leskinen, Risto (b. 21.2.1915), Judicial Delegate to Parliament (Ombudsman) 1962–70, Chancellor of Justice since 1970.

Linna, Väinö (b. 20.12.1920), author. Made his breakthrough by publishing The Unknown Soldier (1954), which describes a machine-gun company during the Second World War. The Unknown Soldier is an exceptional war novel because of its realistic style and its dialogue, written in colourful dialects. In 1959–62 Linna published a three-volume epic on crofters, Täällä Pohjantähden alla (Here under the North Star), on the history of a family from the 1880s till the 1950s. The book offers a cross-section of the Finnish population during that period. Linna was awarded the Literary Prize of the Nordic Council in 1963.

Olavi Mattila

Mattila, Olavi (b. 24.10.1918), Envoy Extraordinary and Minister Plenipotentiary. Worked in the Ministry for Foreign Affairs and the Ministry of Trade and Industry in 1952–64. Managing director of Valmet Oy since 1965, chairman of the board since 1973. Chairman of the board of Enso-Gutzeit since 1973. Minister at the Prime Minister's Office and Deputy Minister for Foreign Affairs 1963, Minister of Trade and Industry 1970, Minister at the Office and Minister of Foreign Trade 1970–71, Minister for Foreign Affairs 1971–72 and 1975.

Veijo Meri

Arto Noras

Paavali

Erkki Palosuo

Reima Pietilä

Laila Pullinen

*Einojuhani
Rautavaara*

Meri, Veijo (b. 31.12.1928) author. One of the most original writers of his generation. He often describes his characters in strange situations with grotesque and often cruel humour without any direct social or historical aims. The most common background is war, which is caricatured in his works. Meri has written novels, collections of short stories, and plays for radio, theatre and television. Meri is the most internationally famous Finnish writer of his generation. His works have been translated into several languages. Meri was awarded the Literary Prize of the Nordic Council in 1973.

Noras, Arto (b. 12.5.1942), celloist. Professor at the Sibelius Academy since 1970. The rich expression and technical brilliance of his playing make Noras one of the most noteworthy celloists of our time.

Paavali (Yrjö Paavali Olmari, b. 28.9.1914), Orthodox Archbishop of Karelia and Finland since 1960. Assistant Bishop of the Finnish Orthodox Church 1955—60.

Palosuo, Erkki (b. 28.6.1912), geophysicist. Director of the ice section of the Finnish Marine Research Institute 1955—72, director of physics section 1972—73, professor of geophysics at the University of Helsinki 1973—77. Specialist in glaciers. The British-owned Palosuo Islands in the Antarctic Ocean were named for him in 1962.

Pietilä, Reima (b. 25.8.1923), architect. Artist professor 1971—73, professor of architecture at the University of Oulu 1973—79. Designed the Dipoli student union at the Helsinki University of Technology (1966), the Kaleva Church in Tampere (1966, in colaboration with his wife, Raili Pietilä), the Hervanna leisure-time and congregation centre and the Hervanna business centre in Tampere, and the centre of the administrative complex in Kuwait.

Pullinen, Laila (b. 21.7.1933), sculptress. Studied in Italy, where she also worked for long periods. Her public works include Daughter of the Sea (Helsinki, 1971), Crescent (Jeddah, 1971—80) and the Flame (Jeddah, 1977—80).

Rautavaara, Einojuhani (b. 9.10.1928), composer, lecturer at the Sibelius Academy 1966—71, professor of composition since 1976. Rautavaara's ample output, rich in nuances, includes the operas The Mine and Apollon and Marsyas, the ballet Temptations, 3 symphonies, a concerto for cello, piano and soprano, the orchestral pieces A Requiem in Our Time and Cantus Arcticus. True and False Unicorn for orchestra and choir, 3 violin quartets, a wind octet, an oboe quartet, 2 piano sonatas, a bassoon and cello sonata, the piano works Fiddlers and Icons, song cycles including the Orpheus sonatas, Vigilia, Book of Life and a Children's Mass for choir.

Rekola, Esko (b. 10.6.1919), chief secretary, Minister of Foreign Trade since 1979. Chief secretary of the Prime Minister's Office 1965−66 and since 1977. Chief director of the Finnish State Railways board of administration 1966−73, secretary general of the Ministry of Communications 1973−76. Minister of Finance 1963−64 and 1976−77, Minister at the Ministry of Finance 1976 and 1977−79.

Esko Rekola

Salama, Hannu (b. 6.10.1936), author. Describes people discriminated against for their socio-political background, living in a collective and loveless atmosphere. His realistic, lively prose is tinged with lyrical beauty when he describes nature. Published several collections of short stories and poems. His works include Juhannustanssit (Midsummer Night's Dance, 1964), which brought on a legal action against him on grounds of blasphemy, and Siinä näkijä missä tekijä (The Price of Dissent, 1972), which describes underground communist activities during the Second World War. Salama was awarded the Literary Prize of the Nordic Council in 1975.

Hannu Salama

Sallinen, Aulis (b. 6.4.1935), composer, professor. Manager of the Radio Symphony Orchestra 1960−70, teacher at the Sibelius Academy 1965−76, chairman of the association of Finnish composers 1971−73. His works include solo pieces for various instruments, chamber music, choral works, solo songs, four symphonies, the ballet Variations sur Mallarmé and the operas The Horseman (1974) and The Red Line (1978). Sallinen was awarded the Nordic Council prize for The Horseman in 1978.

Aulis Sallinen

Sarpaneva, Timo (b. 31.10.1926), designer. Has designed art glass, cast iron pots, stainless steel, textiles and clothing, and worked as the designer of industrial arts exhibitions. Has gained international recognition and awards, e.g. the Lunning Prize (1956). Honorary Doctor at the Royal College of Arts (London) in 1967.

Timo Sarpaneva

Siilasvuo, Ensio (b. 1.1.1922), Lieutenant General. Worked in different posts for the United Nations: in Cyprus 1957, Lebanon 1958, Cyprus 1964−65, assistant commander of the United Nations Truce Supervision Organisation in the Middle East 1967−70, temporary commander 1970, commander 1970−73, commander of

Ensio Siilasvuo

Helvi Sipilä

Heikki Siren

Pentti Somerto

Kalevi Sorsa

Pär Stenbäck

the peacekeeping forces in the Middle East 1973−75, and chief planner of these operations 1975−79.

Sipilä, Helvi (b. 5.5.1915), barrister. Director General of the Finnish Girl Scout Organisation 1952−69, representative of Finland in the UN committee on the status of women 1960−68 and 1971−72, chairman of the United Nations third committee 1971, Assistant Secretary General of the United Nations 1972−80. Secretary General of International Women's Year and the IWY World Conference.

Siren, Heikki (b. 5.10.1918), architect, professor. His works include student dormitories, a chapel and a restaurant building at Otaniemi, the small auditorium of the National Theatre (Helsinki, 1954), the renovation of the Finnish National Theatre (Helsinki, 1962), Lahti Concert Hall (1954), Orivesi Church (1960), Espoo Funeral Chapel (1961), restoration of Helsinki Cathedral (1961−63), residential areas in Hagen and Krefeld in the Federal Republic of Germany (1965) and at Boussy St-Antoine (Paris, 1970), the holiday villages of Lacanau (Bordeaux, 1966), and Hakone (Japan, 1976), Brucknerhaus Concert Hall (Linz, 1973) and Conference Palace (Baghdad, 1978). Most of his work is done in cooperation with his wife Kaija Siren (b. 1920), with whom he has a joint architectural bureau.

Somerto, Pentti (b. 4.12.1927), managing director of the Central Federation of Finnish Employers, barrister. Director of the Finnish Metal Trades Employers' Association 1967−70, assistant managing director of the Employers' Association of Finnish Woodworking Industries 1970−71, director of the Central Federation of Finnish Employers 1971−75, managing director since 1975.

Sorsa, Kalevi (b. 21.12.1930), Social Democratic politican. General secretary of the Finnish Unesco committee 1965−69, assistant head of department of the international section of the Ministry of Education 1967−69. Party secretary of the Social Democratic Party 1969−75, chairman since 1975. Member of Parliament since 1970. Minister for Foreign Affairs 1972 and 1975−76. Prime Minister 1972−75 and 1977−79.

Stenbäck, Pär (b. 12.8.1941), chairman of the Swedish People's Party since 1977, Minister of Education since 1979. Director of the Hanasaari Swedish-Finnish Cultural Centre since 1974. Deputy chairman of the Swedish People's Party 1970−77. Member of Parliament since 1970.

Kari Suomalainen

Ilkka Suominen

Lauri Sutela

Martti Talvela

Suomalainen, Kari (b. 15.10.1920), artist, illustrator and cartoonist. Political cartoonist of Helsingin Sanomat, the largest-circulation daily in Finland, since 1951. Has published several collections of cartoons and a play, A Thorough Scoundrel.

Suominen, Ilkka (b. 8.4.1939), chairman of the National Coalition Party since 1979. Member of Parliament 1970—75.

Kain Tapper

Sutela, Lauri (b. 11.10.1918), General. Head of the General Staff 1968—71, head of the Commander-in-Chief's Staff 1971—74, Commanding General of the Defence Forces since 1974.

Talvela, Martti (b. 4.2.1935), singer. Primary school teacher 1958—60. Has performed at the Royal Opera, Stockholm, 1960—61, Deutsche Oper, West Berlin, since 1962. One of Finland's leading performing artists. Numerous recordings. Important opera roles: Boris Godunov, Philip II (Don Carlos), Sarastro (The Magic Flute), Gurnemanz (Parsifal). Artistic director of the Savonlinna Opera Festival 1972—79.

Pekka Vennamo

Tapper, Kain (b. 6.6.1930), sculptor, artist professor 1972—75. Helsinki Festival artist of the year 1981. Tapper's works are characterized by the mutual interaction of the material (most often wood) and the artist.

Vennamo, Pekka (b. 7.11.1944), chairman of the Rural Party of Finland since 1979. Member of Parliament 1972—75 and since 1979.

Pertti Viinanen

Viinanen, Pertti (b. 9.4.1937), chairman of the Central Organization of Finnish Trade Unions since 1981, third chairman 1976—81. Carter and truck operator 1955—67, employee and wage secretary of the Finnish Paper Workers' Union 1967—76.

Virolainen, Johannes (b. 31.1.1914), Centre Party politician, Doctor of Agriculture and Forestry, farmer.

Johannes Virolaine

108

Lauri Vuorela

Chairman of the Association of Rural Youth 1945–54, chairman of the Centre Party 1964–80. Member of Parliament since 1945, Speaker of Parliament 1966–68 and since 1979. Deputy Minister of the Interior 1950–51, Minister at the Prime Minister's Office 1951, Minister of Education 1953–54 and 1968–70, Minister for Foreign Affairs 1954–56, 1957 and 1958, Minister of Agriculture 1961–63 and 1976–79, Prime Minister 1964–66, Minister of Finance 1972–75.

Paavo Väyrynen

Vuorela, Lauri (b. 27.2.1913), meteorologist. Professor of meteorology at the University of Helsinki 1958–71. Chief director and professor of the Finnish Meteorological Institute 1971–79. Member of the New York Academy of Sciences since 1980, member of the European Academy of the Sciences, Arts and Letters since 1980.

Väyrynen, Paavo (b. 2.9.1946), politician, M.P. since 1970, political secretary to the prime minister 1970–71, vice-chairman of the Centre Party 1972–80, chairman since 1980. Minister of Education 1975–76, Minister of Labour 1976–77, and Foreign Minister 1977–79 and since 1979.

Raino Westerholm

Westerholm, Raino (b. 20.11.1919), chairman of the Christian League of Finland since 1973. Member of Parliament 1973–79.

Wirkkala, Tapio (b. 2.6.1915), industrial art designer, Academician. Wirkkala works in many areas of the industrial arts and the materials he uses include wood, metal, glass and porcelain. Has designed decorative and household objects for domestic and foreign production, and worked as a graphic artist and exhibition architect. Received numerous international awards and honorary mentions, including an honorary doctorate at the Royal College of Art in 1971.

Tapio Wirkkala

von Wright, Georg Henrik (b. 14.6.1916), philosopher. Member of the Finnish Academy since 1961, Professor in Helsinki 1946–61, in Cambridge 1948–51, Chancellor of Åbo Academy 1968–77. Studies issues related to induction and probability, and logical empirism and ethics. Publications include The Logical Problem of Induction (1941), A Treatise on Induction and Probability (1951), An Essay in Model Logic (1951), Logical Studies (1957), The Varieties of Goodness (1963), Norm and Action (1963), The Logic of Preference (1963), An Essay in Deontic Logic (1968), Explanation and Understanding (1971), Causality and Determinism (1979), Freedom and Determination (1980).

G.H. von Wright

Ylppö, Arvo (b. 27.10.1887), doctor of medicine. Professor of Pediatrics at the University of Helsinki 1921—57. Chairman of the Mannerheim League for Child Welfare 1920—60, principal doctor at the Children's Castle Hospital and director of pediatric nursing courses 1920—63. Forerunner in pediatric research and teaching, and children's care and welfare in Finland. Works include studies on infants and premature babies and their illnesses.

Arvo Ylppö

DIPLOMATIC REPRESENTATION

E = Embassy, C = Commercial Section, L = Legation
Country Representation in Finland; Finnish Representation abroad

Afghanistan E: Skatertny Pereulok 25, Moscow; see USSR
Albania E: Tyrgatan 3 A, 114 27 Stockholm; see Rumania
Algeria E: Danderydsgatan 3–5: Fack, S-100 41 26 Stockholm 26;
4, Boulevard Mohammed V, Algiers
Angola E: −; see Zambia
Argentina E: Bulevardi 10 A 14, 00120 Helsinki 12;
Avenida Santa Fé 846, 5° piso, 1059 Buenos Aires
Australia E: Sergels Torg 12, 103 42 Stockholm; 10 Darwin Avenue
Yarralumla, A.C.T. 2600
Austria E: Eteläesplanadi 18, 00130 Helsinki 13;
Untere Donaustrasse 13–15, 1020 Vienna
Bahrein E: −; see Kuwait
Bangladesh E: Zemledelcheski per. 6, Moscow; see India
Barbados E: 6 Upper Belgrave Street, London SWIX 8 AZ;−
Belgium E: Kalliolinnantie 5, 00140 Helsinki 14; Place Stephanie 20, 1050
Brussels
Bolivia E: −; see Peru
Brazil E: Mariankatu 7 A 3, 00170 Helsinki 17; Avenida das Nações. 27
S.E. Sul, 70 417 Brasilia–D.F.
Bulgaria E: Itäinen Puistotie 10, 00140 Helsinki 14; Ul. Frederic
Joliot-Curie 15, 1113 Sofia
Burma E: Ul. Gertsena 41, Moscow; see The Philippines
Burundi: E: Drosselweg 2, 5307 Wachtberg–Niederbachem 6 Bonn; −
Cameroon E: 84, Holland Park, London W 11 3SB; see Nigeria
Canada E: Pohjoisesplanadi 25 B, 00100 Helsinki 10;
222 Somerset St., West Ottawa, Ontario, K2P 2G3
Central African Republic E: 416, Boulevard Lambermont, 1030 Brussels;−
Chile E: Kommendörsgatan 35, 114 58, Stockholm; see Argentina
China E: Vanha Kelkkamäki 9–11, 00570 Helsinki 57; 30, Guang Hua
Lua 30, Peking
Colombia E: Östermalmsgatan 46, 114 26 Stockholm;
C: Carrera 7 No. 35–33, Bogotá D.E.
The Congo People's Republic E: 16–18, Avenue Franklin Roosevelt, 1050
Brussels;−
Costa Rica E: Cromwell Mansions, 225 Cromwell Road, London SW 5;
see Mexico
Cuba E: Mannerheimintie 16 A 12, 00100 Helsinki 10; Avenida 5 ta no
9202 Miramar, Havana
Cyprus E: Ulica Gerzena 51, Moscow; see Israel
Czechoslovakia E: Armfeltintie 14, 00150 Helsinki 15;
Dřevná 2, Prague 2
Denmark E: Yrjönkatu 9, 00120 Helsinki 12; Hammerensgade 5,
1267 Copenhagen K

Ecuador E: Kristian Augustgate 13, Oslo 1; see Peru
Egypt E: Stenbäckinkatu 22 A, 00250 Helsinki 25; 10, El Kamel
  Mohamed Street, Zamalek, Cairo
El Salvador E: –; see Mexico
Ethiopia E: Östermalmsgatan 34, 114 26 Stockholm; Tedla Desta
  Building, Africa Avenue, Addis Abeba
France E: Itäinen Puistotie 13, 00140 Helsinki 14; 2, Rue Fabert, 1 Place
  de Finlande, 75007 Paris
German Democratic Republic E: Vähäniityntie 9, 00570 Helsinki 57;
  Schadowstrasse 6, 108 Berlin
Germany, Federal Republic of E: Fredrikinkatu 61, 00100 Helsinki 10;
  Friesdorferstrasse 1, 5300 Bonn 2
Ghana E: Egebierg Allée 13, 2900 Hellerup, Copenhagen; see Nigeria
Great Britain E: Uudenmaankatu 16–20, 00120 Helsinki 12;
  38 Chesham Place, London SW1X 8 HW
Greece E: Lönnrotinkatu 15 C 26, 00120 Helsinki 12; Eratosthenous 1,
  Athens TT 501
Guatemala E: Zietenstrasse 16, 5300 Bonn 2; see Mexico
Guinea E: Pomerantsev Pereulok 6, Moscow;–
Holy See E: Immortellevej 11, 2950 Vedbaek; Villa Lante,
  Passegiata del Gianicolo 10, 00165 Roma
Honduras E: 48 George Street, London W 1 H5RF; see Mexico
Hongkong E: –; General Consulate: 1409 Hutchinson House,
  10 Harcourt Road, Hongkong; E: see Great Britain
Hungary E: Kuusisaarenkuja 6, 00340 Helsinki 34; Vérhalom utca 12–16,
  Bép, 1023 Budapest II
Iceland E: Kommendörsgatan 35, 114 58 Stockholm; see Norway
India E: Annankatu 15 B 14, 00120 Helsinki 12; 42, Golf Links,
  New Delhi–110003
Indonesia E: Eerikinkatu 37, 0018 Helsinki 18;
  15 A Jalan Kusumah Atmaja, Jakarta
Iran E: Västra Yttringe Gård, Elfviksvägen, Lidingö; 73 Gandhi Avenue,
  Corner of 25th Street, Teheran
Iraq E: Lars Sonckintie 2, 00570 Helsinki 57;
  Hai Babel, House n:o 11, Zuqaq 3, Mahallah 929, Baghdad
Ireland E: Grokholsky per. 5, Moscow; see Netherlands
Israel E: Vironkatu 5 A, 00170 Helsinki 17; 224 Rehov Hayarkon,
  Tel-Aviv 63405
Italy E: Fabianinkatu 29 C 4, 00100 Helsinki 10; Viale G. Rossini 18,
  00198 Roma
Ivory Coast E: Gersonsvej 8, 2900 Hellerup, Copenhagen;
  C: Résidence Pelieu, Avenue Delafosse, Abidjan; E: see Nigeria
Japan E: Yrjönkatu 13, 00120 Helsinki 12; 2–7, 3-chome, Roppongi,
  Minato-ku, Tokyo 106
Jordan E: Sadovskikh Pereulok 3, Moscow; see Lebanon
Kampuchea, Democratic E: –; see China
Kenya E: Birger Jarlsgatan 37, 103 95 Stockholm; Diamond Trust House,
  Moi Avenue, Nairobi
Korea, Democratic People's Republic of E: Kulosaaren puistotie 34
  0057 Helsinki 57; C: Munsudong Block 66, Building 25, Pyongyang; E:
  see China
Korea, Republic of E: Annankatu 16 B 50, 00120 Helsinki 12;

Embassy of Finland, 6th Floor, Kyobo Building, 1–1, 1–ka, Chongro, Chongro-Ku, Seoul

Kuwait E: 3e Neopalimosky per. 13–5, Moscow; Dasman Square, White House No2 5th Floor, Kuwait

Laos E: 5 Palace Green, Kensington, London W8 4QA; see Vietnam

Lebanon E: Sadovo Samotechnaya 14, Moscow; Gefinor Center, Clémenceau Street, Beirut

Lesotho E: Granhøjen 7, 2900 Hellerup, Copenhagen;–

Liberia E:n Fafnervägen 23, 182 64 Djursholm; –

Libya E: Haapaniemenkatu 6, 00530 Helsinki 53; Ammar Ben Yaser Street 9, Tripoli

Luxembourg E: Khruchevsky Pereulok 3, Moscow; see Belgium

Malaysia E: Mosfilmovskaya ul. 50, Moscow; Angkasa Raya Building, 10th Floor, Jalan Ampang, Kuala Lumpur

Malta E: Viktoriastrasse 7, 5300 Bonn 2; see Libya

Mauritius E: 32–33 Elvaston Place, London SW7;–

Mexico E: Pohjoisranta 14 A 16, 00170 Helsinki 17; Plaza Comermex, Piso 9, México 10, D.F.

Mongolia E: Ulica Pisemskogo 11, Moscow; see USSR

Morocco E: Gotenstrasse 7–9, 5300 Bonn 2; 12 rue d'Oran, Rabat

Mozambique E: –; see Tanzania

Nepal E: 12 A Kesington Palace Gardens, London WS 4QU; see India

The Netherlands E: Raatimiehenkatu 2 A 7, 00140 Helsinki 14; Carnegielaan 11, 2517 The Hague

New Zealand E: Ulica Vorovskogo 44, Moscow; see Australia

Nicaragua E: Krysshammarvägen 32, 17157 Solna; see Venezuela

Niger E: Dürenstrasse 9, 5300 Bonn 2;–

Nigeria E: Tyrgatan 8, 114 27 Stockholm; 8–10 Broad Street, Lagos

Norway E: Rehbinderintie 17, 00150 Helsinki 15; Drammensvejen 40, Oslo 2

Oman E: Lindenallee 11, 5300 Bonn 2; see Saudi Arabia

Pakistan E: Ul. Sadova Kudrinskaya 17, Moscow; see Iran

Panama E: Fridhemnsgatan 15, 102 24 Stockholm 12;–

Paraguay E: –; see Argentina

Peru E: Fredrikinkatu 16 A 22, 00120 Helsinki 12; Los Eucaliptos 291, San Isidro, Lima

The Philippines E: Karmanitsky per. 6, Moscow; Bank of Philippine Islands, Corner of Ayala Avenue and Paseo de Roxas

Poland E: Armas Lindgrenintie 21, 00570 Helsinki 57; Fr. Chopina 4/8, 00-559 Warsaw

Portugal E: Itäinen Puistotie 11 B, 00140 Helsinki 14; Rua Miquel Lupi, 12, 1200 Lissabon

Qatar E: Brunnenallee 6, 5300 Bonn 2; see Kuwait

Rumania E: Stenbäckinkatu 24, 00250 Helsinki 25; Strada Atena 2 bis, 71271 Bucharest

San Marino E: –; see Italy

Saudi Arabia E: –; Villa Zogheibi, Sharafiya, Jeddah

Senegal E: Skeppsbron 8, 111 30 Stockholm; see Nigeria

Singapore E: Per. Voyvodina 5, Moscow; see India

Somalia E: Spasopeskovskaya Pl. 8, Moscow; see Tanzania

South Africa E: Rahapajankatu 1 A 5, 00160 Helsinki 16; 171 Esselen Street, Sunnyside, Pretoria

Spain E: Bulevardi 10 A 8, 00120 Helsinki 12; Fortuny 18, Madrid-4
Sri Lanka E: Strandvägen 39, 104 40 Stockholm 14; 35/2 Guildford
  Crescent, Colombo 7
Sudan E: Klara Södra Kyrkogata 1, 115 22 Stockholm; see Egypt
Sweden E: Mannerheimintie 15 A, 00260 Helsinki 26; Regeringsgatan 67,
  111 56 Stockholm
Switzerland E: Uudenmaankatu 16 A, 00120 Helsinki 12;
  Weltpoststrasse 4, 3015 Berne
Syria E: Mansurovsky Peteulok 4, Moscow; see Lebanon
Tanzania E: Oxtorgsgatan 2–4, 11157 Stockholm;
  NIC-Investment House, 9&10 floors, Independence Avenue,
  Dar es Salaam
Thailand E: Sandhamnsgatan 36, 102 51 Stockholm; 89/17 Vithayu Road,
  3rd Floor, Bangkok
Trinidad and Tobago E: 42 Belgrave Square, London SW1X 8 NT; see
  Venezuela
Tunisia E: Drottninggatan 73 C, 111 36 Stockholm; 67, rue Oum
  Khaltoum, 1001
Turkey E: Topeliuksenkatu 3 b A 1–2, 00260 Helsinki 26; Farabi Galip
  Dede Sokak 1/20, Çancaya, Ankara
Uganda E: Sofievej 15, 2900 Hellerup; see Kenya
United Arab Emirates E: Godesberger Allee 125–127, D 5300 Bonn 2; see
  Saudi Arabia
Uruguay E: Kommendörsgatan 35, 114 58 Stockholm; see Argentina
USA E: Itäinen Puistotie 14 A, 00140 Helsinki 14; 3216 New Mexico
  Avenue N.W. Washington D.C. 20016
USSR E: Tehtaankatu 1 B, 00140 Helsinki 14;
  Kropotkinsky Pereulok 15/17, Moscow G-34 119034
Venezuela E: Mannerheimintie 18, 00100 Helsinki 10; C: Centro Plaza,
  Torre C, Piso 18, Avenida Francisco de Miranda, Los Palos Grandes,
  Caracas
Vietnam, Socialistic Republic of E: Örby Slottsväg 26, 125 36 Älvsjö;
  Bâtiment e 1, Quartier Diplomatique, Trung Tu, Hanoi
Yugoslavia E: Kulosaarentie 36, 00570 Helsinki 57;
  Bircaninova 29, 11 000 Belgrade
Zaire E: Klara Södra Kyrkogatan 1, 111 52 Stockholm;–
Zambia E: Klara Södra Kyrkogatan 1, 111 52 Stockholm; Chanik House,
  4th floor, Sapele Road, off Lusaka Square, Lusaka
Zimbabwe E: –; see Zambia

Permanent Missions of Finland to the United Nations:
  866 United Nations Plaza, New York, N.Y. 10017, USA
  149 A, Route de Ferney, 1218 Le Grand-Saconnex, Geneva, Switzerland

BIBLIOGRAPHY

General Works of Reference

Finland. Facts and Figures. 2nd ed. Helsinki: Otava, 1979. 239 p.
Finland Handbook. 1981. 16th ed. Helsinki: Finnish Tourist Board et al., 1980. 168 p.
Finnish Museums. Ed. by A-T. Huovinen. Helsinki: Finnish Museums Association, 1979. 121 p. (Finnish Museums Association. Publications 18.)
Nicol, G., Finland. London: B.T. Batsford, 1975. 216 p.

Geography, Guide books, Illustrated Works

Boehm, D.A., Finland in Pictures. 13th ed. New York, NY: Sterling Publishing, 1977. 64 p. (Visul Geography Series.)
Carlander, G. & Bergendahl, C., Finn Guide to Helsinki. Helsinki: Finnish Travel Association, 1979. 133 p.
Finland. Geneva: Nagel Publishers, 1980. 367 p. (Nagel's Encyclopedia Guide.)
Finlandia. Pictures of Finland. Text K. Siikala. Helsinki: Kirjayhtymä, 1981. 104 p. Text in English and French.
Häyrinen, U. & Linkola, M., Lapinmaa. Four Seasons in Lapland. Foreword by U. Kekkonen. Helsinki: Kirjayhtymä, 1975. 191 p. Text in English, Finnish and German.
Jones, M., Finland. Daughter of the Sea. Folkestone: Dawson, 1977. 247 p.
Marsden, W., Lapland. Amsterdam: Time-Life International, 1976. 183 p.
Mead, W.R. & Jaatinen, S.H., The Åland Islands. New Abbot: David & Charles, 1975. 183 p.
Nickels, S., The Traveller's Guide to Finland. London: Jonathan Cape, 1977. 240 p.
Pitkänen, M. & Napola, J., Suomalainen järvi. Finland – a Land of Lakes. 2nd ed. Helsinki: Weilin+Göös, 1980. 157 p. Text in English, Finnish, German and Swedish.
Roininen, V., Löydä vanha, kaunis Helsinki. Beautiful Old Helsinki. Helsinki: Werner Söderström, 1981. 157 p. Text in English, Finnish, French, German and Swedish.
Suomen nähtävyydet. The Sights of Finland. Editor & texts V. Mäkinen. 2nd ed. Helsinki: Werner Söderström, 1980. 868 p. Text in English, Finnish, German and Swedish.

Suomi. Finland. Helsinki: Kansankulttuuri & Leipzig:
VEB F.A. Brockhaus Verlag, 1975. 152 p. Text in
English, Finnish, German and Russian.

History, Politics, Society

Burnham, R.E., Who Are the Finns. A Study in
Prehistory. Reprint. London: Faber & Faber, 1979.
90 p.

Condon, R.W., The Winter War. Russia against
Finland. New York, NY: Ballantine Books, 1972. 160
p. (Ballantine's Illustrated History of the Violent
Century. Campaign Book 24.)

The Finnish Parliament. Ed. & ill. by J. Jäppinen.
Jyväskylä: Gummerus, 1979. 95 p.

The Finnish Legal System. Ed. by J. Uotila. Helsinki:
Union of Finnish Lawyers, 1966. 263 p. (Publications
of the Union of Finnish 26.)

Erfurth, W., The Last Finnish War. Washington, DC:
University Publications of America, 1979. 252 p.

Irwin, J.L., The Finns and the Lapps. How They Live
and Work. 2nd ed. London: David & Charles, 1978.
171 p.

Jakobson, M., Finnish Neutrality. London: Hugh
Evelyn, 1968. 125 p.

Jutikkala, E. & Pirinen, K., A History of Finland. New
and rev. ed. London: Heineman, 1979. 253 p.

Kekkonen, U., Neutrality. The Finnish Position.
London: Heineman, 1973. 258 p.

(Kekkonen, U.) Urho Kekkonen. A Statesman for
Peace. Ed. by K. Korhonen. Helsinki: Otava &
London: Heineman, 1975. 186 p.

Kirby, D.G., Finland in the Twentieth Century. London:
C. Hurst, 1979. 253 p.

Klinge, M., 60 Years Independent Finland. Helsinki:
Otava, 1977. 79 p.

Maude, G., The Finnish Dilemma. Neutrality in the
Shadow of Power. London: Oxford University Press,
1976. 153 p.

Matheson, D., Ideology, Political Action and the
Finnish Working Class. Helsinki: Societas scientiarum
Fennica, 1979. 191 p. (Commentationes scientiarum
socialium 10.)

Nousiainen, J., The Finnish Political System.
Cambridge, MA: Harvard University Press, 1971.
454 p.

Puntila, L.A., The Political History of Finland
1806–1966. 2nd ed. Helsinki: Otava & London:
Heineman, 1975. 248 p.

Rintala, M., Four Finns. Political Portraits of Four
Major Leaders of the Finnish Government:
Mannerheim, Tanner, Ståhlberg and Paasikivi.

Berkeley, CA: University of California Press, 1969.
120 p.
Screen, J.E.O., Mannerheim. The Years of Preparation.
London: C. Hurst, 1970. 158 p.
Sinnemäki, M., The Church in Finland. Helsinki:
Kirjaneliö, 1978. 40 p. Text in English, German and
Swedish.
Upton, A.F., The Finnish Revolution. Minneapolis, MN:
University of Minnesota Press, 1981. 600 p.
Westermarck, N., Finnish Agriculture. 4th ed. Helsinki:
Kirjayhtymä, 1969. 83 p.

Finnish Language

Aaltio, M-H., Finnish for Foreigners. 1−2. 10th ed.
Helsinki: Otava, 1978−1981.
Atkinson, J., A Finnish Grammar. 5th ed. Helsinki:
Finnish Literature Soolety, 1981. 131 p.
Kallioinen, V., Finnish Conversational Exercises.
Elementary Level. Helsinki: Finnish Literature
Society, 1974. 169 p.
Whitney, A.H., Finnish. A Comprehensive Course for
Beginners. 5th ed. London: Hodder & Stoughton,
1979. 301 p. (Teach Yourself Books.)

Dictionaries

Alanne, V.S., Suomalais-englantilainen suursanakirja.
Finnish-English General Dictionary. 3rd ed. Helsinki:
Werner Söderström, 1980. 1111 p
Hurme, R. & Pesonen, M., Englantilais-suomalainen
suursanakirja. English-Finnish General Dictionary.
2nd ed. Helsinki: Werner Söderström, 1978. 1181 p.
Wuolle, A., Englantilais-suomalainen opiskelusanakirja.
English-Finnish Dictionary. Helsinki: Werner
Söderström, 1978. 512 p
Wuolle, A., Suomalais-englantilainen opiskelusanakirja.
Finnish-English Dictionary. Helsinki: Werner
Söderström, 1979. 484 p
Wuolle, A., Suomi-englanti-suomi. Taskusanakirja.
Finnish-English-Finnish. Pocket Dictionary. 5th ed.
Helsinki: Werner Söderström, 1980.

Art, Architecture

(Aalto, A.) Alvar Aalto 1898−1976. Ed. by A.
Ruusuvuori. Helsinki: Museum of Finnish
Architecture, 1978. 168 p.
Aalto, A., Complete Work. 1−3. München:
Artemis/KNO, 1970−1978. Text in English, French
and German.

Aalto, A. Synopsis. Painting, Architecture, Sculpture. 2nd ed. Basel & Boston & Stuttgart: Birkhäuser Verlag, 1980. 240 p. (History and Theory of Architecture 12.) Text in English, French and German.

Boulton-Smith, J., The Golden Age of Finnish Art. Helsinki: Otava, 1976. 180 p.

Boulton-Smith, J., Modern Finnish Painting. London: Weidenfeld & Nicolson, 1970. 126 p.

Fields, J. & Moore, D., Finland Creates. Text by Pekka Suhonen. 2nd ed. Jyväskylä: Gummerus, 1980. 131 p. Text in English and Finnish

Kruskopf, E., Sam Vanni − ikkuna Eurooppaan − Window on Europe. Helsinki: Weilin+Göös, 1978. Text in English, Finnish and Swedish.

Kruskopf, E. & Pietinen, O., Eila Hiltunen. Helsinki: Otava, 1976. 95 p.

Pearson, P.D., Arvar Aalto and the International Style. New York, NY: Watson-Guptill Publications, 1978. 240 p.

Richards, J.M., 800 years of Finnish Architecture. Newton Abbot: David & Charles, 1978. 191 p.

Salokorpi, A., Modern Architecture in Finland. London: Weidenfeld & Nicolson, 1970. 128 p.

Santakari, E. & Savolainen, I., Keskiajan kivikirkot. The Medieval Stone Churches of Finland. Helsinki: Otava, 1979. 175 p. Text in English, Finnish and Swedish.

Sarpaneva, T. & Bruun, E. & Kruskopf, E., Finnish Design 1875−1975. Helsinki: Otava, 1975. 116 p.

Schildt, G., Modern Finnish Sculpture. London: Weidenfeld & Nicolson, 1970. 64 p.

(Sonck, L.) Lars Sonck. Architect. Ed. by J. Pallasmaa. Helsinki: Museum of Finnish Architecture, 1981. 156 p. Text in English and Finnish.

Suolahti, E., Helsinki. City in a Classic Style. 2nd ed. Helsinki: Otava, 1980. 63 p.

Waltari, M. & Rácz, I., Aimo Kanerva. In Search of the Image of the Finnish Landscape. 2nd ed. Helsinki: Weilin+Göös, 1978. 87 p. Text in English and Finnish.

Willcox, D.J. & Hector, O., Finnish Design. Facts and Fancy. New York, NY & Toronto: Van Nostrand Reinhold Company & Helsinki: Werner Söderström, 1973. 157 p.

Literature, Music, Theatre

Ahokas, J.A., History of Finnish Literature. Bloomington, IN: Indiana University, 1973. 568 p. (Indiana University Publications. Uralic and Altaic Series 72.)

Cowie, P., Finnish Cinema. London: Tantivy Press,

1976. 128 p. Finnish Theatre Today. Ed. by K.
Veltheim & I. Tainio. Helsinki: Finnish Centre of the
International Theatre Institute (ITI), 1971. 71 p.

Haltsonen, S. & Puranen, R., Kaunokirjallisuutemme
käännöksinä. [Translations of Finnish literature.
Novels, short stories, poetry, plays. Bibliographical
guide.] Helsinki: Finnish Literature Society, 1979.
150 p. (Suomi 122:4)

Helistö, P., Finnish Folk Music. Helsinki: Foundation
for the Promotion of Finnish Music, 1973. 30 p.

Helistö, P., Music in Finland. Helsinki:
Finnish-American Cultural Institute, 1980. 77 p.

Hillier, J., Cinema in Finland. London: British Film
Institute, 1975. 67 p.

Kalevala. Transl. by W.F. Kirby. London: Everyman's
Library, 1978. 285 p.

Modern Nordic Plays. Finland. New York, NY: Twayne
Publishers, 1973. 304 p. (Library of Scandinavian
Literature 17.)

Mäkinen, T. & Nummi, S., Musica Fennica. Helsinki:
Otava, 1965. 139 p.

Niemi, A.A., The quest of the Sampo. New York, NY:
Vantage Press, 1978. 127 p.

Richards, D., Music of Finland. London: Hugh Evelyn,
1968. 120 p.

Salmenhaara, E., Sibelius and Ainola. Helsinki: Werner
Söderström, 1976. 41 p. Text in English and Finnish.

Savutie, M., Finnish Theatre. Helsinki: Otava, 1980. 63
p.

Sermilä, J., Finland's Composers. Helsinki: Ministry for
Foreign Affairs, 1976. 25 p.

Tawaststjerna, E., Sibelius. 1. 1865–1905. London:
Faber & Faber, 1976. 316 p.

Territorial Song. Contemporary Writing from Finland.
Selected and transl. by H. Lomas. London: London
Magazine Editions, 1981. 157 p.

Finnish Food, Sauna

Hollander, C., How to Build a Sauna. New York, NY:
Sterling Publishing, 1979. 128 p.

Johnson, T. & Miller, T., The Sauna Book. New York,
NY: Harper & Row, 1977. 197 p.

Let's Have a Sauna. Text M. Herva. Helsinki: The
Finnish Sauna Society, 1980. 22 p.

Ojakangas, B., The Finnish Cookbook. 9th ed. New
York, NY: Crown Publishers, 1964. 250 p.

Syö hyvin Helsingissä. Where to Eat in Helsinki. Publ.
by the Gastronomic Society of Finland. 2nd ed. Espoo:
Tietoteos, 1981. 157 p. Text in English and Finnish.

Viherjuuri, M. & Tanttu, A-M. & Tanttu, J., Finlandia
Gastronomica. A Guide to Finnish food. 4th ed.
Helsinki: Otava, 1981. 61 p. (Finland for Foodlovers.)

TRAVEL INFORMATION

New York	Finland National Tourist Office, 75 Rockefeller Plaza, New York, N.Y. 10019
London	Finnish Tourist Board UK office, Finland House Annexe, 66/68 Haymarket, London SW1Y 4RP
Paris	Office National du Tourisme de Finlande, 13 rue Auber, 75009 Paris
Amsterdam	Fins Nationaal Verkeersbureau voor de Benelux, Stadhouderskade 69 1072 AD Amsterdam
Stockholm	Finska Turistbyrån, Birger Jarlsgatan 35, 111 45 Stockholm
Copenhagen	Finlands Turistbureau, Vester Farimagsgade 6, 1606 Köbenhavn V
Oslo	Finlands Turistkontor, Lille Grensen 7, Oslo 1
Hamburg	Finnisches Fremdenverkehrsamt, Rothenbaumchaussee 11, (Curio-Haus), 2000 Hamburg 13
München	Finnisches Fremdenverkehrsamt, Franzstrasse 5/lr, 8000 München 40
Zürich	Finnische Zentrale für Tourismus, Schweizergasse 6, 8001 Zürich
Helsinki	Finnish Tourist Board, Kluuvikatu 8, 00100 Helsinki 10